"Who is Jesus, really, and why does he matter? That's the question Rebecca tackles in this insightful exploration of the life of Jesus, using his four authorized biographies—the Gospels. For the last two thousand years, those who have studied Jesus have found him simple enough for a child to understand yet profound enough to confound the philosophers. Whether you're exploring who Jesus really is for the first time or just want to learn more about the beauty of our Savior, *Confronting Jesus* is a must read."

J. D. Greear, Pastor, The Summit Church, Raleigh-Durham, North Carolina; author, *Just Ask*

"In a time when the public witness of the church in America has been profoundly damaged due to scandals, divisions, and culture wars, I have encouraged so many of my friends—from non-Christian neighbors to church planters—to return to the simplicity and the power of Jesus. Albert Einstein once admitted that though he wasn't a believer in Jesus, he was nevertheless 'enthralled by the luminous figure of the Nazarene.' There couldn't be a better time than now for us all to be enthralled by him once more, and I can't think of a better person to (re)introduce us to the luminous figure of the Nazarene than Rebecca. A beautiful and moving book!"

Abraham Cho, Senior Director of Training, City to City NYC and North America

"Among the many books that have been written about Jesus, *Confronting Jesus* is one of the most carefully written, compelling, and convincing volumes I have seen. What makes it special is how thoughtful and accessible it is, not only to Christians but also to those who have questions or even doubts concerning faith. If you are looking for a resource to help you or a friend encounter and consider Jesus Christ as he really is, look no further. This is that resource."

Scott Sauls, Senior Pastor, Christ Presbyterian Church, Nashville, Tennessee; author, *A Gentle Answer* and *Beautiful People Don't Just Happen*

"McLaughlin offers anyone curious about or interested in Christianity the best entry point by giving her readers a high-definition look at Jesus: who he is, what is unique and significant about him, and most importantly, why it's worth believing in him. The descriptions of Jesus you will find in this book come together to make an attractive and compelling case for why so many of us love and follow him."

Vermon Pierre, Lead Pastor, Roosevelt Community Church, Phoenix, Arizona

"No one has been more impacted by the phenomenon of 'fake news' than Jesus Christ. The amount of misinformation circulated about this first-century Jewish man is staggering. In *Confronting Jesus*, Rebecca masterfully unpacks what the Gospels reveal about Jesus. You will be amazed by the good news he delivered, in awe of the life he lived, and compelled by the invitation he extends."

Christine Caine, Founder, A21 and Propel Women

"It is no secret that Jesus is the central figure in the Christian faith. However, we live in a day when many do not know why he is so central. Rebecca McLaughlin has done us a kindness by laying out the beauty of Jesus with clarity and conviction. Bring your questions and, through these pages, find Jesus ready, willing, and able to answer."

Irwyn L. Ince Jr., Coordinator, Mission to North America; author, *The Beautiful Community: Unity, Diversity, and the Church at Its Best*

Confronting Jesus

Other Crossway Books by Rebecca McLaughlin

Confronting Christianity: 12 Hard Questions for the World's Largest Religion

10 Questions Every Teen Should Ask (and Answer) about Christianity

Confronting Jesus

9 Encounters with the Hero of the Gospels

Rebecca McLaughlin

WHEATON, ILLINOIS

Confronting Jesus: 9 Encounters with the Hero of the Gospels

Published by Crossway
1300 Crescent Street
Wheaton, Illinois 60187

Cover design: Josh Dennis, Jordan Singer

First printing 2022

Printed in the United States of America

All emphases in Scripture quotations have been added by the author.

Trade paperback ISBN: 978-1-4335-8113-7
ePub ISBN: 978-1-4335-8116-8
PDF ISBN: 978-1-4335-8114-4
Mobipocket ISBN: 978-1-4335-8115-1

Library of Congress Cataloging-in-Publication Data

Names: McLaughlin, Rebecca, 1980– author.
Title: Confronting Jesus : 9 encounters with the hero of the gospels / Rebecca McLaughlin.
Description: Wheaton, Illinois : Crossway, 2022. | Includes bibliographical references and index.
Identifiers: LCCN 2021050694 (print) | LCCN 2021050695 (ebook) | ISBN 9781433581137 (trade paperback) | ISBN 9781433581144 (pdf) | ISBN 9781433581151 (mobipocket) | ISBN 9781433581168 (epub)
Subjects: LCSH: Jesus Christ—Person and offices—Biblical teaching. | Bible. Gospels—Criticism, interpretation, etc.
Classification: LCC BT203 .M3755 2022 (print) | LCC BT203 (ebook) | DDC 232—dc23/eng/20211118
LC record available at https://lccn.loc.gov/2021050694
LC ebook record available at https://lccn.loc.gov/2021050695

Crossway is a publishing ministry of Good News Publishers.

LB 31 30 29 28 27 26 25 24 23 22
15 14 13 12 11 10 9 8 7 6 5 4 3 2 1

For Julia,
who generously read drafts of this manuscript twice,
and for everyone else who does not believe that Jesus is the Son of God,
but will take the time to read this book

Contents

Preface

I WROTE MY FIRST BOOK while pregnant with my third child. But its true gestation was much longer. I'd spent almost a decade working with Christian professors at leading universities in the United States and Europe. I'd heard their stories and how their research and their faith were not in conflict but were intertwined—especially in areas that are supposed to have discredited historic Christianity.

I'd spent even longer interacting with non-Christian friends who had principled objections to my faith. They found it not only implausible but also in important ways immoral. Not only, for example, had science disproved the existence of God, but the church's track record when it came to racism, to women, and to the treatment of people who identify as LGBT made them uninterested in even considering Jesus. I wrote *Confronting Christianity: 12 Hard Questions for the World's Largest Religion* as a love letter to these friends. I got their questions and concerns but wanted to explain as best I could that, when we look more closely, every seeming roadblock to faith in Jesus becomes a signpost.

I wrote the book that's in your hands as something of a sequel. It doesn't focus on the questions that keep people from considering Jesus. Instead, it looks straight at Jesus himself. If you feel curious about Jesus, this book is for you. If you feel like you need to hear a lot of answers to your reasonable questions before you want to spend your time exploring Jesus as revealed in the Gospels, I'd be honored if you'd read *Confronting Christianity*.

My thirdborn is now three, and he's exploring Jesus for himself. He and his big sisters recently learned a verse from the Gospel of John, in which Jesus says, "I am the light of the world. Whoever follows me will not walk in darkness, but will have the light of life" (John 8:12). This is the kind of claim that Jesus makes about himself. If it's not true, this book is worthless, and I'm stumbling around in darkness. But if it *is* true, I pray that you will find yourself attracted to the light.

Introduction

ON MY FIRST NIGHT out after giving birth to my third child, I saw *Hamilton*. I was the only Brit in the group. My American companions could enjoy the story of rejecting British rule a little differently. But even I could relish the pacey, punchy, hip-hop history of a man of whom I'd previously not heard. Hamilton was once one of the least known Founding Fathers. But now, this nonstop, shot-taking, revolution-making immigrant is one of the most famous figures in American history.

When it comes to the Bible's four accounts of Jesus's life, we find the story of another history maker who was born poor and obscure. But rather than shaping just America, this man's impact has been felt across the world. Like *Hamilton* writer Lin-Manuel Miranda, the Gospel authors were writing about a real, historical person, and their goal was to tell his story in a way that would energize their audience. But unlike Miranda, the Gospel writers claim to report the actual words and deeds of Jesus, not just to capture the spirit of their hero. The New Testament Gospels known as Matthew, Mark, Luke, and John are four of the best-selling books of all time. But many of us have not sat down to read even one of them cover to cover.

Perhaps your knowledge of Jesus is like my knowledge of Alexander Hamilton before I saw Miranda's musical. You know the basic outline: a first-century Jewish man, known as Jesus Christ, was born to a virgin named Mary and was believed to be God's Son. He was seen as a miraculous healer and a great moral teacher, and although he was ultimately crucified by the Romans, Christians believe that he was raised from the dead. Perhaps you know some of his most famous quotes: "Don't judge" or "Love your neighbor as yourself." But that's about it. You haven't seen the show. Or maybe you know more. Perhaps you grew up in the church, hearing Jesus quoted and reading the Bible, but you've moved on since then. You can hum along to Jesus's highlight hits. But some of the details of his life have become a little hazy over time, and honestly, you wonder if the Gospels are mostly mythical accounts about a fairy story figure from two thousand years ago.

In this book, we'll explore what the Gospels tell us about Jesus, and we'll ask how they might be relevant to our own lives today. In chapter 1 ("Jesus the Jew"), we'll look at the history of the Jewish people prior to Jesus's birth, the evidence for his existence as a real human being, the political context in which he was born, and the evidence that the Gospels are reliable sources for his life and teachings. In chapter 2 ("Jesus the Son"), we'll examine what the Gospels say about Jesus's divine identity. In chapter 3 ("Jesus the King"), we'll explore Jesus's claim to be God's long-promised, everlasting King. In chapter 4 ("Jesus the Healer"), we'll see how Jesus's healing miracles illuminated his identity. In chapter 5 ("Jesus the Teacher"), we'll notice how Jesus's teachings both ground and disrupt our modern, moral paradigms. In chapter 6 ("Jesus the Lover"), we'll uncover Jesus's claim to be the true bridegroom to God's people and the perfect friend. In chapter 7 ("Jesus the Servant"), we'll see how Jesus takes a servant role and calls his followers to do so too. In chapter 8 ("Jesus the Sacrifice"), we'll explore the paradoxical claim that Jesus is both the sacrificial Lamb of God and the temple where the sacrifice is made. Finally, in chapter 9 ("Jesus the Lord"), we'll confront Jesus's claim that he is rightful Lord of all and that our truest freedom will be found in serving him. By the end, I hope you'll want to read a Gospel for yourself to find out more about this first-century Jewish man who claimed he was the maker of all things, the King of the Jews, the mighty healer, the greatest teacher, the ultimate lover, the suffering servant, the perfect sacrifice, and the universal Lord.

In most Broadway shows, the staging hides the lighting. But in *Hamilton* the lights are deliberately laid bare. This book attempts a similar approach. Each chapter draws on all four Gospels, but rather than just providing a composite image, my hope is that the book will make you curious about the particular angle from which each Gospel shines its light.

Let's start with the stage set up.

Mark's Gospel was likely written first: around thirty-five to forty-five years after Jesus's death. It's believed to be based on the memories of Simon Peter—one of Jesus's closest friends—written down by a man named John Mark.[1] (As we'll see in our tour through the Gospels, lots of people at that time had two names!) Mark is the shortest Gospel, and it's bursting with a Hamilton-like immediacy that fits with the impulsive character of Peter himself. In fact, the Greek word for "immediately" forms the drum beat of Mark's Gospel, as if the writer were running out of time!

1 The claim that Mark was acting as Peter's interpreter and scribe appears in very early writings—for example, by Papias, Bishop of Hierapolis, writing early in the second century.

Matthew's Gospel is traditionally associated with one of Jesus's disciples: a tax collector known as Levi or Matthew. Matthew records the famous "Sermon on the Mount"—a concentrated dose of Jesus's teachings, snatches of which you'll likely know even if you've never read his Gospel. It is the most unmistakably Jewish account of Jesus's life, continually connecting Jesus to Old Testament texts. But Matthew continually weaves in non-Jewish figures, and it ends with Jesus commanding his first Jewish disciples to go and make disciples of all nations (Matt. 28:19–20)

Luke's Gospel begins by explaining his process. Like a careful historian, Luke has interviewed "those who from the beginning were eyewitnesses," and he has written up their testimony into "an orderly account" (Luke 1:2–3). In Luke we find a particular focus on women, the poor, the weak, the sick, and the marginalized. Luke was a doctor and the only non-Jewish Gospel author. The book of Acts, which tells the story of the early Christian movement, was written by Luke as a sequel to his Gospel.

The last Gospel to be written down was John, likely sixty or so years after Jesus's death. It's more philosophical in tone—more like an opera than a musical. John skips many incidents in the other Gospels and includes others that don't feature elsewhere. But as we'll see in chapter 1, we can't dismiss John as historically unreliable because it was written later. Some of the most respected scholars believe that this Gospel was written by one of Jesus's first followers, who as a young man witnessed much of what he records.[2]

2 See, e.g., D. A. Carson, *The Gospel according to John* (Grand Rapids, MI: Eerdmans, 1991), 68–81; Richard Bauckham, *Jesus and the Eyewitnesses: The Gospels as Eyewitness Testimony* (Grand Rapids, MI: Eerdmans, 2006), 6; Craig L. Blomberg, *The Historical Reliability of the New Testament: Countering the Challenges to Evangelical Christian Belief* (Nashville: B&H Academic, 2016), 153–59.

You can read even the longest Gospel (Luke) in the time it takes to watch *Hamilton*, and just as I enjoyed Miranda's musical in the company of friends, you might find it helpful to read a Gospel with a friend or two as well: maybe with a friend who sees Jesus differently than you do. Perhaps together you can try to account for his rise to the top: how this man who lived poor and died young—who never wrote a book, raised an army, or sat on a throne—became the most life-transforming, earthshaking, history-making human of all time.

1

Jesus the Jew

THE 2017 MOVIE *The Zookeeper's Wife* begins with a mother watching her young son nap. Two animals lie with him. At first, I thought they must be piglets. But as the camera moved from soft focus to clarity, I realized that they were baby lions. The early scenes depict an almost literally Edenic life. This woman, Antonina, walks fearlessly into the elephant enclosure to resuscitate a newborn calf. With one hand, she clears the baby's airways. With the other, she calms its anxious mother, who could have trampled her at any time. The love that binds her to her husband, Jan, flows out into their love for their creatures. But from the first, we know this scene is set in Warsaw and the date is 1939. When Jan has no choice but to help some little Jewish kids to board a train, we know where they are going. As he pulls Jews out of the ghetto and hides them in the basement of their zoo, we know what fate awaits them if they're found.[1] The film is arrestingly beautiful, but the horror of the Holocaust is continually pressing in. I had to pause it multiple times to weep.

1 *The Zookeeper's Wife*, directed by Niki Caro (London: Scion Films, 2017).

Likewise, when it comes to the Gospel accounts of Jesus's life, the story of the Jewish people saturates the text. But for many of us, the contours of that story are unknown. We know what happened after Jesus's life on earth, but not before. We're so used to Jesus's unrivaled impact on the world that it's hard for us to see him as he first stepped onto the stage of human history. We're so used to the dominance of Christianity—which is now the largest and most diverse belief system in the world—that it's hard for us to imagine Jesus as a member of a subjugated ethnic group. We're so used to Jesus's influence on Western culture that it's hard for us to remember his profoundly Middle Eastern roots. We're so used to Christianity that we forget how deeply Jewish Jesus is.

In this chapter, we'll glimpse where Jesus came from: literally, politically, and theologically. We'll ask whether Jesus was a real man, who worked and walked and wept two thousand years ago, and whether we should see the Gospels as historical accounts that can truly give us access to Jesus the Jew. But first, we'll excavate the ancient history of the Jewish people. When Jesus walked onto the stage, it wasn't act one. It was the first scene after the intermission. So we'll begin with a whirlwind, snatch-and-grab tour of the plot of the Bible up to that point, and we'll start to notice the ways in which Jesus's story is best understood in light of Jewish history.

In the Beginning

For many in the West today, believing that there is one true Creator God who made the universe can seem implausible. Not believing that there is a God at all is seen by many as the default setting. You'd need real evidence to believe in a Creator. In the ancient Near East, the Jewish belief in only *one* Creator God was also highly countercultural. But the alternative wasn't atheism or agnosticism;

it was polytheism. Most people believed in many gods. Against this majority view, the Bible's first chapter boldly proclaims that there is only one Creator God, who made all things, and who made human beings in his image (Gen. 1:26–27).

The global success of Christianity has made belief in one Creator God the most widespread view across the world today. (The proportion of people who don't believe in a Creator is actually much smaller than many in the West assume, and the proportion is shrinking globally, not growing!) But both at the time when Genesis was written and at the time when Jesus was born, monotheism would not have seemed plausible. To make the claim still more preposterous, the Gospels insist that Jesus *is* this one Creator God: not a demigod, or another god, but the one true God made flesh. So why would this Creator God become a man? The first three chapters of the Bible's first book set a scene that makes us long for a solution.

Genesis 2 paints a picture like the opening of *The Zookeeper's Wife*: human beings in loving relationship with each other, charged with caring for the rest of God's creation. But while for Jan and Antonina, hatred, sin, and death invaded from *outside*, in Genesis 3 the rot comes from *within*. God's prototypic people break God's prototypic law. This ruins their relationship with God and with each other. Like an asteroid strike ravaging the atmosphere, their turn away from God spoils everything. But just as the *The Zookeeper's Wife* takes us from Eden through pain and death and heartache to redemption, so God was working in the darkness to unfold his life-restoring plan—a plan to bring human beings back into intimate relationship with God and with one another, a plan that hinged on Jesus.

God's plan began with a promise to a quite unpromising man who came from a city that in modern-day terms is in Iraq. Abraham was old and childless. But God promised to make him into a great nation and to bless all the families of the earth through his family (Gen. 12:1–3). And Abraham believed God. Well, eventually. Like many figures in the Bible's cast, Abraham hit some spectacular fails. But in the end, he believed. His wife Sarah got pregnant and their son Isaac was the seed from which the Jewish people grew. Both Matthew and Luke offer genealogies to show that Jesus was descended from Abraham (Matt. 1:1–17; Luke 3:23–38). Jesus's Jewish identity is vital to his mission in the world.

Isaac married Rebekah (which is a brilliant name), and they had two sons: Jacob and Esau. Jacob was renamed Israel, and his twelve sons started Israel's twelve tribes. In another stunning fail, one of the twelve sons, Joseph, was sold into slavery by his brothers. But as Joseph later explained to them, what they intended for evil, God intended for good (Gen. 50:20). Joseph became overseer of Egypt under Pharoah and saved both Egypt and his family from famine. He married an Egyptian woman, and their two half-Egyptian sons became founders of the half-tribes of Ephraim and Manasseh. So from the beginning of the twelve tribes of Israel, people from different ethnicities were spliced into God's covenant people. These are the first murmurings of the fulfillment of God's promise to bless all the families of the earth through Abraham's family. But after four hundred years in Egypt, the Israelites had gone from being honored immigrants to subjugated slaves.

The Birthing of a Nation

After helping hundreds of African Americans escape slavery, Harriet Tubman was nicknamed "Moses." It was a fitting moniker. Tubman had experienced slavery herself before leading others out of it, and the original Moses had experienced oppression as a baby—when

Pharoah had ordered the death of all the Israelite baby boys—but went on to lead the Israelites out of Egypt. Moses only escaped by being hidden in a basket that was floated on the Nile and found by Pharaoh's daughter, who raised him. But when God called Moses from a supernaturally burning bush, he'd been living away from Egypt for years. Moses made every excuse he could think of as to why he *shouldn't* go back and demand that Pharoah let God's people go. But the God of the universe didn't take no for an answer.

When Moses asked for God's name, he replied, "I AM WHO I AM. . . . Say this to the people of Israel: 'I AM has sent me to you'" (Ex. 3:14). The God of the Bible is the one who simply *is*. But he also identifies himself with his people: "I am the God of your father, the God of Abraham, the God of Isaac, and the God of Jacob" (3:6). The one who *is*, is Israel's promise-making God. The enigmatic divine name, *Yahweh*, that appears in the Old Testament is a form of the Hebrew verb "to be" used in the expression "I AM." For Jews, the name *Yahweh* was so holy that it was never read aloud. They substituted "Adonai," which means "my Lord." This was later carried over into the Greek translation of the Old Testament, which rendered *Yahweh* with the Greek word *kurios*—that is, "Lord." Following this practice, most English translations of the Bible substitute "the LORD," using small capital letters, for *Yahweh*. But as we'll see in chapter 2, Jesus does an utterly outrageous thing: he takes this divine name—"I am"—upon himself.

When Moses told Pharoah to let God's people go, Pharaoh refused. So God sent ten horrific plagues. Pharoah kept agreeing to let the Israelites go but then changing his mind. The last plague echoes the slaughter of the Israelite boys from which Moses himself had escaped. Moses warned Pharaoh that if he still refused, the firstborn child in every house would die. The Israelites were told to daub the blood of a lamb on their doorposts so that death would pass over their homes. Here, as in many Old Testament moments, we have a foreshadowing of Jesus, who (as we'll see in chapter 8) is hailed in the Gospels as the Lamb of God: the one who's sacrificed like a Passover lamb, so that everyone who trusts in him can live.

At last, Pharaoh consented to let God's people go. But then he changed his mind again and sent his armies to pursue the Israelites—trapped between their enemies and the Red Sea. In a final act of rescue, God sent a great east wind to part the sea. His people walked across, before the waters closed back on their pursuers. This moment of release—the exodus—became the birthing of a nation. In some respects, it stood in Israel's memory like the War of Independence in the minds of my American friends. "We roll like Moses," sings Hamilton, "claiming our promised land."[2] But instead of fighting their own battles, the Israelites had been fought for by God. And unlike America, ancient Israel had a unique relationship with God. The Jews of Jesus's day were clinging to this hope. Despite oppressive Roman rule, they still believed that they were God's own people: descended from Abraham, rescued from slavery, and—just as importantly—given the law.

The Rules of the Relationship

When my husband complains that I've stolen his favorite hoodie or charger or keys (I'm quite the conjugal kleptomaniac), I parrot back our wedding vows: "All that I am I give to you, and all that I have I share with you." Marriage frees me up to take my husband's stuff. But it severs other freedoms. I've turned away

2 Lin-Manuel Miranda, "My Shot," on *Hamilton: Original Broadway Cast Recording*, Atlantic Records, 2015.

from every other possible spouse to bind myself to him. He's done the same. This vow of exclusivity is not designed to stunt the relationship but to protect it.

After Yahweh rescued the Israelites from Egypt, he gave them the law to show how to live with him. The first of his famous Ten Commandments reads, "I am the LORD your God, who brought you out of the land of Egypt, out of the house of slavery. You shall have no other gods before me" (Ex. 20:2–3). Like wedding vows, God's law established the norms of the relationship. Worshiping God alone came first, and from it flowed a wealth of other moral acts: like loving others as yourself, providing for the poor, defending the oppressed, living in sexual faithfulness, and speaking the truth. But even while Moses was receiving these divine commands, God's people were breaking them by worshiping a golden calf.

As the story of Israel unfolds, we see this pattern again and again: God's people turn from him. They worship idols and oppress the poor. So God sends judgment. They repent. He rescues them. The cycle starts again. Like a serially unfaithful spouse, God's people kept violating the rules of the relationship. We'll see in chapter 5 that Jesus lived and taught God's law in radical and life-affirming ways, and in chapter 6 we'll see how Jesus stepped into the shoes of Yahweh, the faithful husband to his all-too-often unfaithful people, and how his coming finally dealt with the intractable problem of their sin—a problem that was frequently made worse by their leaders.

Kings and Catastrophes

One of my favorite *Hamilton* songs is, "You'll Be Back." It is a comic pseudo love song, sung by the deranged British monarch, that features the timeless lyric, "Da da da dat da dat da da da da ya da."[3] It's not an attractive depiction of royalty. From the American perspective, King George is just a subjugating, tax-demanding nuisance. For a thousand years after they entered God's promised land, the Israelites had leaders and judges, but no king. When they requested one, God told them that a human king might not be all they hoped for. In fact, the description God gives of how a king would treat them is not unlike the depiction of King George in *Hamilton* (see 1 Sam. 8:10–18). But God consented to the people's plea, and Israel's first king, Saul, was anointed.

Saul began well, but ended badly. He disobeyed God, and God rejected him. Saul's replacement, King David, started as a shepherd boy who famously defeated the gigantic Philistine, Goliath. God called David "a man after his own heart" (1 Sam. 13:14), and David wrote many of the stunning Old Testament psalms. He was the archetypal king of Israel, and Jesus (who descended from him) is often hailed as "Son of David" in the Gospels. And yet, like so many of the scriptural would-be heroes, David had his own spectacular fails. One day he saw a beautiful woman bathing on a roof, summoned her to sleep with him, and then when she got pregnant arranged for her husband to die in battle. God sent a prophet to expose David's sin, and he mournfully repented. But still, his moral failure and his role in Israel's wars meant he could not be the one to build God's temple. That fell to his son Solomon.

Solomon was known for his God-given wisdom. But even he could not escape the cycle of sin. Like the pagan kings around him, he started a harem and ended up worshiping many gods. We'll see in chapter 3 that Jesus is the long-promised, ultimate King of

3 Jonathan Groff, vocalist, "You'll Be Back," by Lin-Manuel Miranda, on *Hamilton: Original Broadway Cast Recording.*

the Jews, who alone could rule with justice. But we'll also see in chapter 8 that Jesus is the real temple: the place where God would truly dwell and where the real sacrifice was made.

After Solomon's death, the land was split into a northern kingdom (Israel) and a southern kingdom (Judah), and the cycle continued. Like a loving father, God sent prophet after prophet to call his people back and warn them of impending judgment. But finally, the hammer fell. In 725 BC the northern kingdom, Israel, fell to the Assyrians. The king of Israel and many of the people were exiled. Then, in 597 BC, Jerusalem (in the southern kingdom of Judah) was captured by the Babylonians. Its leaders were exiled. Ten years later, Jerusalem and the temple were destroyed, and many of the people were deported. "By the waters of Babylon," one of the psalms laments, "there we sat down and wept, when we remembered Zion" (Ps. 137:1).[4]

By the time of Jesus's birth, God's people had been allowed to return to their land and to rebuild their temple. But rather than being sovereign, they were living as a subjugated race. And yet, faithful Jews were clinging to their scrolls and hoping God would send the Savior-King he'd promised by his prophets. But so far, every hope had been destroyed.

Enter Jesus.

Jesus of Nazareth

If you scrolled back two thousand years, you would not have zoomed in on Nazareth as the likely hometown of the most influential man in all of history. First-century Israel was a backwater of

4 Zion was the name of the fortified hill in Jerusalem that King David conquered, renamed "the city of David," and took as his residence (see 2 Sam. 5:6–9). Later Old Testament writers often used the term *Zion* to refer to Jerusalem—the capital city that served as the site of the Lord's temple and the king's throne.

the Roman Empire, and Nazareth was a backwater of Israel. When one of Jesus's followers, Philip, told a fellow Jew, Nathanael, "We have found him of whom Moses in the Law and also the prophets wrote, Jesus of Nazareth, the son of Joseph," Nathanael replied, "Can anything good come out of Nazareth?" (John 1:45–46). It was a good question.

Nazareth was a marginal town in a troubled area. In 4 BC a group of Jews in the region rebelled against Rome and captured the Roman armory in Sepphoris, a town four miles from Nazareth.[5] The Romans retaliated. They burned Sepphoris to the ground, sold its inhabitants into slavery, and crucified about two thousand Jews.[6] This was the world in which Jesus was raised. Resisting Roman rule bought you a one-way ticket to a cross.

Things could have been worse. The Romans generally tolerated Jewish religious practices. King Herod, who was not ethnically Jewish, was installed by Rome as "King of the Jews" in 37 BC and enjoyed significant autonomy to rule—including remodeling the temple in Jerusalem to make it one of the most impressive buildings of its day. But Herod never really won his subjects' hearts. He was a brutal man, even having several of his own sons executed, and is best remembered in Matthew's Gospel for ordering the slaughter of the baby boys and toddlers of Bethlehem (Matt. 2:16). In the decades following Herod's death, multiple Jewish freedom fighters attempted insurrections against Rome.

When Jesus began his public ministry, likely in the late 20s, he was stepping into a political landscape that was already highly charged. Hamilton declared, "I will lay down my life if it sets us

5 Both Matthew and Luke say that Jesus was born during the reign of King Herod, who died in 4 BC, so our traditional dating of Jesus's birth to AD 1 is likely a few years off.

6 The Jewish historian Josephus reports this in his *Jewish Antiquities* 17.10.

free,"[7] and like many other would-be Messiahs, Jesus died nailed to a Roman cross. But unlike any other leader of the day, his life and teachings changed the world. Or so we've been told. But how can we know that Jesus even existed, let alone that the stories we have in the Gospels are true?

In his 2012 book, *Did Jesus Exist? The Historical Argument for Jesus of Nazareth*, New Testament scholar Bart Ehrman answers the first question for us like this: "The reality is that whatever else you may think about Jesus, he certainly did exist."[8] Ehrman is a skeptic when it comes to Jesus's divinity. But he says the view that Jesus is a real, historical figure "is held by virtually every expert on the planet."[9] We know this not just from the Bible itself but from multiple early references to Jesus from people who didn't like Christians at all. They confirm that Jesus was a first-century Jewish rabbi, was claimed to be "the Christ" (God's promised King), was crucified under Pontius Pilate (the Roman Governor of Judaea), and was subsequently worshiped by his followers.

The real life of Jesus the Jew—a human being, born in history—is vital to every other claim presented in the Gospels or narrated in this book. He cannot be the other things the Gospels claim if he is not a real, historical figure, with flesh and blood like you and me. But believing that Jesus of Nazareth was a Jewish man in history is not enough for us to have any confidence that what the Gospels say about Jesus is true. So in the rest of this chapter, we're going to address some of the legitimate questions twenty-first-century readers might have about the historical reliability of the Gospel

7 Miranda, "My Shot."

8 Bart D. Ehrman, *Did Jesus Exist? The Historical Argument for Jesus of Nazareth* (New York: HarperOne, 2012), 4.

9 Ehrman, *Did Jesus Exist?*, 4.

accounts. Because if the Gospels are more like myth than history, then Christianity is a sophisticated fake: like a supposedly ancient manuscript that turns out to be a forgery.

Weren't the Gospels Written Too Long after Jesus's Death?

In 2020 civil rights leader Rev. John Perkins interviewed civil rights lawyer Bryan Stevenson. The son of a sharecropper, Perkins was born in poverty in Mississippi but fled to California at age seventeen after his brother was murdered by a town marshal. In 1957 he became a Christian and decided to go back to his hometown to share the good news of Jesus. His subsequent role in the Civil Rights Movement earned him harassment, imprisonment, and beatings. Bryan Stevenson was born two years after Perkins's conversion, in a poor, black, rural community in Delaware. The Civil Rights Movement made it possible for him to make his way to Harvard Law School. But poor black Americans were still facing grave injustice, and Stevenson founded the Equal Justice Initiative in Alabama to represent people who had been sentenced to death on flimsy evidence or without proper representation. When Perkins asked his guest to share how God called him to his work, Stevenson told the story of his first visit to death row. A law student intern, he'd been sent to tell a prisoner that he was not at risk of execution in the coming year. Stevenson felt unprepared. The prisoner had chains around his ankles, wrists, and waist. Stevenson delivered his message, and the man expressed profound relief. They talked for hours. But then two officers burst in.

Angry that the visit had taken so long, the officers reapplied their inmate's chains with force to punish him. Stevenson pleaded with the officers to stop. He told them it was his fault they'd overrun their time. But the prisoner told Stevenson not to worry. Then he planted his feet, threw back his head, and sang:

> I'm pressing on the upward way,
> New heights I'm gaining ev'ry day;
> Still praying as I'm onward bound,
> "Lord, plant my feet on higher ground."

"Everybody stopped," Stevenson recalled. "The guards recovered, and they started pushing this man down the hallway. You could hear the chains clanking, but you could hear this man singing about higher ground. And in that moment God called me. That was the moment I knew I wanted to help condemned people get to higher ground."[10] When Stevenson told Perkins this story, it was thirty-seven years since he had heard this inmate sing: bang in the middle of the time range most scholars estimate between Jesus's death and the writing of Mark's Gospel.

Jesus's life and ministry had many witnesses—from the crowds that gathered to hear him, to the small group of disciples who had left their homes to follow him. Like actors learning scripts, first-century disciples learned their rabbi's teachings. After Jesus's death, they went on tour, repeating the message and teachings of Jesus to anyone who'd listen. Along with his twelve official disciples, Jesus had many other followers, including many women who traveled with him (see Luke 8:2–3). Some of Jesus's followers are named in the Gospels, and world-class New Testament scholar Richard Bauckham has argued convincingly that these named witnesses are

10 See "Dr. John M. Perkins Bible Study with Bryan Stevenson," YouTube video, June 9, 2020, https://www.youtube.com. The quoted hymn is "I'm Pressing on the Upward Way" by Johnson Oatman Jr. (1856–1922).

being cited as sources for eyewitness testimony. It was like saying, "I got this from Mary Magdalene; she saw it with her own eyes."[11]

None of us remember *everything* that happened years ago. But all of us recall the things that utterly transformed our lives. Stevenson remembered his first visit to death row in detail: the words he said, the things he felt, how the prisoner looked, what the officers did. This day reset his life. Likewise, those who witnessed Jesus were changed forever. They dedicated the rest of their lives to telling his story. Thirty, forty-five, or even sixty years would not have wiped their memories away, any more than John Perkins could forget his experiences in the Civil Rights Movement, some sixty years ago. So, why weren't the Gospels written down sooner? Bauckham argues that they were written decades after Jesus's death precisely because the first eyewitnesses were starting to die out.[12] Like contemporary biographers, the Gospel authors wanted to ensure the eyewitness testimony was preserved with accuracy before it was too late.

How Do We Know We Have the Right Gospels?

Dan Brown's novel *The DaVinci Code* is one of the bestselling books of all time.[13] A pseudo-sequel, *The Lost Symbol*, is now a Peacock TV series.[14] Both books trade in conspiracy theories about the Bible. In particular, *The DaVinci Code* popularized the claim that the New Testament Gospels were picked for political reasons to smother a more feminist version of Jesus that's seen in other so-called Gospels—like the Gospel of Thomas, the most-often-referenced competitor to the biblical Gospels. But if we look at

11 See Richard Bauckham, *Jesus and the Eyewitnesses: The Gospels as Eyewitness Testimony* (Eerdmans, 2006), 39–66

12 See Bauckham, *Jesus and the Eyewitnesses*, 7, 308–9.

13 Dan Brown, *The DaVinci Code* (New York: Doubleday, 2003).

14 Dan Brown, *The Lost Symbol* (New York: Doubleday, 2009).

the evidence, we'll find that the selection of Gospels included in the Bible wasn't arbitrary or politically motivated. Unlike the Gospels in our Bibles, the Gospel of Thomas wasn't written until the mid-to-late second century—far beyond the lifetime of Jesus's disciple Thomas or any other eyewitness. Unlike the Gospels, it's not a biography but a collection of supposed sayings of Jesus. And if you read it, you won't find a more feminist take but rather some quite misogynistic lines, which sound utterly unlike the Jesus of the Gospels.

Some people claim that the four Gospels were only selected at the Council of Nicaea in AD 325. But this is simply false. A few New Testament letters were debated as late as this.[15] But the Gospels were recognized as faithful and authoritative from very early on.[16] Indeed, despite his own skepticism, Bart Ehrman assures us that the four New Testament Gospels are "the oldest and best sources we have for knowing about the life of Jesus" and that this is "the view of all serious historians of antiquity of every kind, from committed evangelical Christians to hardcore atheists."[17] But we don't have the original manuscripts of Matthew, Mark, Luke, and John, so how can we know that the texts we have today are accurate?

How Do We Know We Have the Right Texts?

The first verse of Mark's Gospel reads, "The beginning of the gospel of Jesus Christ, the Son of God" (Mark 1:1). Or does it? The phrase "the Son of God" does not appear in some of the earliest remaining

15 For example, James, 2 Peter, and Jude.

16 Moreover, though discussions took place in the early church about which documents to include in the New Testament, there is no historical evidence (contrary to popular belief) that the Council of Nicaea even discussed this topic.

17 Bart D. Ehrman, *Truth and Fiction in The Da Vinci Code* (Oxford: Oxford University Press, 2004), 102

manuscripts—and even our earliest manuscripts are likely copies of the originals, or even copies of copies. What's more, there are around 400,000 textual differences among the Greek New Testament manuscripts we have. So, are we naïve to think the Gospel texts in our Bibles capture what the Gospel authors wrote? No.

First, the 400,000 textual differences sum up all variants in *all* the approximately 5,600 copies of New Testament texts that we have from the first thousand years after Jesus's death—regardless of when the manuscript was written, how significant the variant is, and how many manuscripts have it. In his insightful book, *Why I Trust the Bible*, New Testament scholar William Mounce gives an example. In Greek, a proper name like Jesus could stand by itself or could be paired with a definite article. If one scribe wrote "the Jesus" in one place in his manuscript when all the others just wrote, "Jesus," that would be counted as a variant—despite making no meaningful difference to the text. The large number of variants in surviving Gospel manuscripts is not because the texts are so unreliable but because we have *so many* manuscripts. What's more, because the manuscripts we have come from so many different places, we can check them for accuracy by triangulating among manuscripts that would have been copied independently and seeing where they do and don't converge.[18]

To be clear, there are *some* places where Gospel texts are in doubt. But none of them affects our understanding of Jesus. For example, while the original first sentence of Mark may not have included "the Son of God," that title is applied to Jesus at other points in Mark and in the other Gospels. The few debated passages are flagged in our modern editions. For example, the last twelve verses of Mark's

18 William D. Mounce, *Why I Trust the Bible* (Grand Rapids, MI: Zondervan, 2021), 134.

Gospel are typically included in our Bibles with the note, "Some of the earliest manuscripts do not include 16:9–20." This is no cover-up job. Like expertly excavated archeological sites, the four Gospels in our Bibles give us faithful access to those early writings about Jesus.

Tragically, this hasn't always been the case. For example, during the Nazi era in Germany, the Gospels in many German Bibles were edited to remove all the references to Jesus's Jewishness and to make his teaching sound supportive of Nazi aggression. The authentic Gospels were completely incompatible with Hitler's ideology, so they had to be changed.[19] Just as white Christians today must reckon with the ways in which our forbears in the faith have been complicit in oppressing folks of African descent, so non-Jewish Christians must reckon with the history of anti-Semitism that has plagued the Western church. But just as racial oppression is torn to shreds by the authentic New Testament texts, so anti-Semitism is utterly irreconcilable with Jesus in the Gospels, who is unquestionably Jewish and most of whose first followers were Jewish too.

What about the Differences between the Gospels?

Six years before he was interviewed by John Perkins, Bryan Stevenson published his best-selling autobiography, *Just Mercy: A Story of Justice and Redemption.* In the introduction, Stevenson tells the story of his first time on death row. The basics are the same as in the interview mentioned above. But there are differences. In the book, Stevenson names the prisoner: Henry. In the interview, he

19 For an overview of Nazi-era Bibles, see Susannah Heschel, *The Aryan Jesus: Christian Theologians and the Bible in Nazi Germany* (Princeton, NJ: Princeton University Press, 2010), 106–10.

never does. In the book, he gives many details of the day and of the conversation he and Henry had that he doesn't mention in the interview. But he also leaves things out in the book that he does say to John Perkins. Most notably, in the interview Stevenson says he felt called by God as Henry sang. In the book, he writes, "In that moment, Henry altered something in my understanding of human potential, redemption, and hopefulness."[20] He doesn't mention God at this point in the book at all. Why did Stevenson tell the story differently to Perkins? Had he forgotten the inmate's name? Was he lying when he said God called him to his work? No. He was addressing a different audience.

If you read the Gospels in quick succession, you'll find a lot of overlap, but also differences. John skips many stories in Matthew, Mark, and Luke and tells us tales found nowhere else. Sometimes the Gospels tell their stories in a different order, or report Jesus's teachings with different words, or in different places. Some of these discrepancies are easily explained: a traveling rabbi would naturally tell similar stories in different places, so if two Gospels record Jesus saying something essentially similar but differently worded, it doesn't mean that one of them is wrong. Other differences arise from the divergent perspectives of the eyewitnesses consulted. If Henry had been interviewed about his first meeting with Stevenson, he might have left out the roughness of the guards, his chains, and his own song. The things that struck the intern on his first death row visit may not have registered for the inmate. It's also likely that Jesus preached in Aramaic—the mother tongue of most Jews in his region—while the Gospels are written almost entirely in Greek: the common language of

20 Bryan Stevenson, *Just Mercy: A Story of Justice and Redemption* (New York: One World, 2014), 12.

the broader culture. Different Gospels may translate an Aramaic teaching differently.

Other Gospel differences arise from simplification and cultural translation. In a talk I've given multiple times to different audiences, I tell the story of a Nigerian street preacher, Oluwole Illisanmi, being arrested outside a tube station in London in 2019. For American audiences, I say "train station" rather than using the British term "tube." Sometimes I comment that the officers were white, but other times I leave this detail out. I claim the two officers gave him a choice: go away or be arrested. But only one of the officers actually said those words. Honestly, I could omit the other officer completely without changing the story. Likewise, we sometimes find two people or two angels in one Gospel story, and only one in another. This doesn't mean one author is wrong; it means one simplified.

As Gospel readers, we are also stepping into a storytelling culture that's different from ours. I recently caught up with a Nigerian friend who told me about an older pastor she revered. She used the pronoun "they," and I assumed she meant the pastor and his wife. But later she explained that Nigerians use plural pronouns to refer to respected elders. I had no idea. Likewise, there are times when the Gospel authors shape their narratives in ways that would have worked in their cultural context but cause confusion in ours: for example, they might order their material theologically rather than chronologically, telling their stories in a particular sequence to make a theological point.

Like stage lights shining from different angles, the Gospel authors write from different eyewitness accounts and with different audiences in mind. My grandpa will sometimes start telling a story and then get interrupted by my grandma. He might be using too much detail ("You don't have to tell them *all of that*") or too little ("No, Julie saw it first, *then* Chris!"). My grandpa will pause and purse his lips and then explain that he *knows* my auntie Julie saw it first, but as Chris is *my* mother, and he's telling the story to *me*, he's focusing on Chris's testimony.

I can imagine how the conversation would have gone if Matthew, Mark, Luke, and John had gathered for a writers' group. Mark's feedback to the others would be, "Speed it up, guys!" Matthew would say, "I hate to break this to you, but you left out most of the ways in which our Lord fulfilled the Scriptures!" Luke would chime in, "I think you've underemphasized quite how much Jesus cares about the poor," and John would say, "Thank God I'm here to tell all the stunning stories you guys left out!" If Stevenson could tell the story of his own calling in two quite different ways for different audiences, we shouldn't be surprised to find the different Gospel authors shedding different light on the life of Jesus of Nazareth: a Jewish man who lived and died in history and whose short life and troublemaking teachings shook the world.

So What?

Toward the end of *The Zookeeper's Wife*, a Nazi officer goes down into the basement of the zoo. The Jews who have been hiding there have gone. But he sees the little Stars of David one young girl has drawn across the walls, with illustrations of her fellow fugitives. The pictures tell a story of their history, their hiding place, and their escape, but most of all their Jewishness.

As we explore the Gospels in this book, we'll find marks of Jesus's Jewishness on every page. Like little Stars of David painted on the basement walls, we'll see connections to the history of Israel at every turn, and we'll see marks of the first-century, Jewish context in which Jesus lived. To understand the Gospels, we must recognize that Jesus was a Jewish man whose real life was played out on a very Jewish stage: a stage whose actors saw themselves as people of the one Creator God, awaiting God's Messiah, who would make God's ancient promises come true.

And so, the curtain rises.

2

Jesus the Son

IN THE EPISODE "A Good Man Goes to War," the British sci-fi hero Doctor Who prepares to fight. His pregnant best friend Amy Pond has been abducted by his enemies, so the Doctor summons all his friends to help. They come. Except for one. The mysterious River Song (who like the Doctor travels in time and space) does not show up. At first the Doctor thinks he's rescued Amy and her daughter. But then the infant in Amy's arms disintegrates. It was only a flesh-avatar of the real baby, who has been kidnapped. Then, as they grieve their terrible mistake, River appears.

> RIVER. Well then, soldier, how goes the day?
> DOCTOR. Where the *hell* have you been? Every time you've asked, I have been there. Where the hell were you today?
> RIVER. I couldn't have prevented this.
> DOCTOR. You could have tried.

The Doctor looks in River's eyes and asks, "Who *are* you?" River sees the crib, where Amy's baby had been sleeping: "Oh, look, your cot! Haven't seen that in a *very* long while." But the Doctor grabs her wrist, "No, no, you tell me. Tell me who you are." Moving his hand to the crib, she says, "I *am* telling you." At last the Doctor understands who River is: she is the future of the baby they've just lost.[1]

The question of Jesus's identity is as vital to the plot of the Gospels as River's identity is to the plot of this episode. The answer is even more incredible. In this chapter, we'll see that all four Gospels claim that Jesus is the Son of God made flesh: the true Creator of the universe in human form. At times they make the claim explicity. But often when someone demands that Jesus tell them who he is, he answers like the enigmatic River Song: "I *am* telling you."

Extraordinary Origins

River's parents, Amy and Rory, were normal human beings. But as they wondered how they'd managed to produce a superhuman, time-traveling daughter, they realized she'd been conceived while they were flying in the Doctor's time-and-space machine. The Doctor is a Time Lord, who not only hops around in time and space, but can also "regenerate" when you or I would just have died. River has these self-same qualities. That's why the Doctor's enemies have kidnapped her. Even in her infancy, they know how powerful River is. Both Matthew's and Luke's Gospels give us accounts of Jesus's conception and birth with similar effect: they help us see who Jesus is and why he has extraordinary, supernatural powers.

Luke gives us the most detailed account, including a conversation Jesus's mother, Mary, had with an angel. The angel told her that she

1 *Doctor Who*, series 6, episode 7, "A Good Man Goes to War," written by Stephen Moffat, aired June 4, 2011, on BBC One.

was going to have a baby, that she should name him Jesus, and that he would be called "the Son of the Most High" (Luke 1:31–32). Mary asked how this would happen, since she was a virgin. The angel explained, "The Holy Spirit will come upon you, and the power of the Most High will overshadow you; therefore the child to be born will be called holy—the Son of God" (1:35).

This news is wild. In the Old Testament, there are multiple instances of God enabling infertile women to conceive. But a virgin being made pregnant by God himself is unprecedented. Unlike the Greek and Roman gods who not infrequently came down to sleep with human beings—producing demigods and heroes—the God of the Bible is utterly transcendent. He'd stated his love for his people again and again, but the Creator God—the one who simply *is*—was totally unlike the pagan gods who intermingled with humanity. And yet Luke claims that by his Holy Spirit, this everlasting God of all the universe had somehow fathered one small human being, who was famously laid in a manger (an eating trough for animals) because there was no room at the inn.

Matthew tells us the story from Joseph's perspective. Mary and Joseph were betrothed: a more binding equivalent to our modern-day engagement. But then Mary was "found to be with child from the Holy Spirit" (Matt. 1:18). Joseph was about to divorce her (betrothal was so serious that reversing it was a form of divorce), but then he met an angel in a dream. The angel explained that Mary's baby was not from another man but from God's Holy Spirit. He told Joseph to name the baby Jesus—which means "Yahweh saves"—and explained, "for he will save his people from their sins" (1:21). Then Matthew makes this curious remark:

> All this took place to fulfill what the Lord had spoken by the prophet:

"Behold the virgin shall conceive and bear a son,
and they shall call his name Immanuel" (which means,
God with us). (1:22–23)

This is one of my favorite biblical non sequiturs. The baby is called *Jesus* not *Immanuel.* But this is Matthew's point. Jesus ("Yahweh saves") and Immanuel ("God with us") amount to the same thing. Our sin has cut us off from God, but Jesus who is fully God and fully man—the one who in himself is "God with us"—has come to save us from our sin and bring us back into relationship with God. Like River placing the Doctor's hand on the crib, when it comes to Jesus's divine identity, Matthew *is* telling us.

If (like me) you learned about the Big Bang growing up, you'll likely have lost your wonder at the idea that the entire universe was once upon a time compressed into a tiny dot of unimaginable density. Likewise, if you grew up celebrating Christmas, you may not be astonished by the totally outrageous claim that the God of all the universe was once upon a time made flesh in embryonic form. But if there *is* a God who made all things, it's not irrational to think he could make one human in a different way. In fact, it would be illogical to think he couldn't. It would be like saying to Simone Biles, "I know you're the greatest gymnast of all time, but I bet you can't do a somersault."

Conceived by God's Holy Spirit, Jesus is not *just* a man. And yet he *is* a man. He's no flesh avatar, whose body could go "pop" like the fake baby in *Doctor Who*. He's every bit as human as you and me. The Bible insists that there is only one Creator God. And yet the Gospels claim that this Creator God became a man, whose dusty sandals needed to be tied and who began, like you and me, in embryonic form. What's more, the stories Luke and Matthew tell of Jesus's conception illuminate the strange Christian claim that the one Creator God exists as three united persons: Father, Son, and Spirit. This same Father-Son-Spirit relationship gets lit up from a different angle in the first chapter of Mark.

Get Ready

In the opening scene of *Hamilton*, multiple characters give snippets of description about the show's hero until finally Aaron Burr asks, "What's your name, man?" At that moment, the spotlight reveals Hamilton himself as he sings, "Alexander Hamilton."[2] The first scene of Mark's Gospel unfolds in a similar way. Drawing together snippets from the prophet Isaiah, the book of Exodus, and the prophet Malachi, Mark writes,

> Behold, I send my messenger before your face,
> who will prepare your way,
> the voice of one crying in the wilderness:
> "Prepare the way of the Lord,
> make his paths straight." (Mark 1:2–3)

Mark identifies this messenger as John the Baptist (1:4). Then he writes, "In those days Jesus came from Nazareth in Galilee" (1:9). Mark has introduced a messenger preparing the way for Yahweh himself ("the Lord") and then had Jesus enter. In a more subtle way than Matthew or Luke, when it comes to Jesus's divine identity, Mark *is* telling us.

John the Baptist makes clear he is the warm-up act, just getting people ready for the main show: "After me comes he who is mightier

2 Lin-Manuel Miranda, "Alexander Hamilton," on *Hamilton: Original Broadway Cast Recording*, Atlantic Records, 2015.

than I, the strap of whose sandals I am not worthy to stoop down and untie. I have baptized you with water, but he will baptize you with the Holy Spirit" (Mark 1:7–8). John the Baptist is so much less important than the coming Lord that he's not even worthy to untie his shoes. And yet, this coming Lord has human feet. John dunks people into water as an act of spiritual washing, but Jesus will immerse them in the Holy Spirit. When Jesus is baptized, the heavens are torn open, God's Spirit descends on Jesus like a dove, and a voice from heaven says, "You are my beloved Son; with you I am well pleased" (1:10–11). This is the spotlight from above, as Jesus enters center stage.

Mark makes no mention of Jesus's miraculous conception. Does this suggest, as some have claimed, that the virgin birth was made up later? I don't think so. Mark is by far the shortest Gospel and skips many events in Jesus's life. But rather than Mark not telling us that Jesus is God's Son, he just expresses it another way: a voice from heaven saying, "You are my beloved Son" (1:11). Like Mark, the last Gospel to be written down makes no mention of Jesus's divine conception. But the claim in John's Gospel that Jesus is divine is the most unmistakable yet.

Let's Start at the Very Beginning

In *The Sound of Music*, Maria famously declares that the very beginning is a very good place to start. The writer of John's Gospel would agree. Instead of starting with Jesus's conception, he starts with the conception of the universe itself. The Bible begins, "In the beginning, God created the heavens and the earth" (Gen. 1:1). John riffs on those world-birthing words:

> In the beginning was the Word, and the Word was with God, and the Word was God. He was in the beginning with God. All

> things were made through him, and without him was not any thing made that was made. In him was life, and the life was the light of men. The light shines in the darkness, and the darkness has not overcome it. (John 1:1–5)

With one hand, John grabs the live wire of the Jewish assertion that Israel's God spoke nothingness into reality, light into the darkness, all things into being. With the other, he grasps the claim of Greek philosophers that there was a universal reason or *logos*—here translated "Word"—that was eternal, unchanging, and present from creation. John touches these two live wires together to present Jesus as the Word who was with God and who *was* God from the beginning. The everlasting one through whom all things were made has now stepped into his own creation. "The Word became flesh and dwelt among us," John writes, "and we have seen his glory, glory as of the only Son from the Father, full of grace and truth" (1:14).

Like Matthew, Mark, and Luke, John's Gospel tells us in its own distinctive way that Jesus is the one true God made flesh. He tells us that no star in the sky or creature on earth was made without the Word who became flesh in Jesus Christ. This means that you and I were made by Jesus too. If this is true, it means that Jesus knows you—embryo to grave, back to front, head to toe, thought to thought. It means he knows you better than you know yourself, because he made each inch of you. In the Old Testament, God's glory is described as being so intense that human beings could not see God and still live. But John claims to have seen this glory in the person of Jesus, who came to live with us. John captures the relational nature of God by explaining that this everlasting Word both was *with* God and *was* God. We'll get more of a glimpse of what it means for Jesus to be "God the Son"—who with the Father and the Spirit together is the one true God—as we continue our tour through the Gospel texts. But first we must ask, is it true, as some suggest, that Jesus *himself* never claimed to be God?

Blasphemy!

In the classic, comic film *The Princess Bride*, Buttercup has been rescued by a masked man who claims he is the Dread Pirate Roberts. Buttercup grew up with a servant boy called Westley, who expressed his love for her in three repeated words: "As you wish." Roberts tells Buttercup that he killed her Westley. "I can't afford to make exceptions," he explains. "Once word leaks out that a pirate has gone soft, people begin to disobey you, and then it's nothing but work, work, work, all the time." So Buttercup pushes him down a ravine, saying, "You can die too, for all I care!" But as the man tumbles down the slope he calls out, "As . . . you . . . wish!" Buttercup cries, "Oh my sweet Westley, what have I done?" and throws herself after him.[3]

In Mark 2:1–2, Jesus is preaching to a packed house. Four friends drag a paralyzed man up onto the roof, cut a hole, and lower him into the room. Seeing their faith, Jesus says to the man, "Son, your sins are forgiven" (Mark 2:5). Imagine his confusion. This man had come for healing, not forgiveness. But the religious leaders known as scribes were horrified: "Why does this man speak like that? He is blaspheming! Who can forgive sins but God alone?" (2:7). The scribes aren't wrong: the only person with the right to say these words is God himself. Jesus's words, "your sins are forgiven," claim an identity as surely as Westley's "As you wish."

Then Jesus asks the scribes, "Which is easier, to say to the paralytic, 'Your sins are forgiven,' or to say, 'Rise, take up your bed

3 *The Princess Bride*, directed by Rob Reiner (Los Angeles: 20th Century Fox, 1987).

and walk'?" (2:9) In one sense, the answer is obvious. Forgiveness won't show physically, so Jesus could save face by claiming it had happened. But rather than choosing A or B, Jesus does both: "'But that you may know that the Son of Man has authority on earth to forgive sins'—he said to the paralytic—'I say to you, rise, pick up your bed, and go home'" (2:10–11).

Immediately, the man got up, picked up his bed, and walked. For Jesus, healing someone's body was easy. As we read on, we find that forgiving sins is hard: it cost Jesus his life. But in this early scene, Jesus proves he has the right to do what only God himself can do.

He *is* telling us.

Who Is This?

Last week, I went to see *Shang-Chi and the Legend of the 10 Rings*. I'm a sucker for fast-paced action films, and this one was fantastic. In one of its most brilliant scenes, a guy named Shaun and his best friend Katy are taking the bus to work. (They're valet parkers.) But then a random thug approaches Shaun and demands in Chinese that he hand over his cool, green necklace. Shaun refuses. Other thugs encircle him. Katy interjects, "You have the wrong guy! Does he look like he can fight?" But then they attack, and Shaun fights back. As the first thug flies through the air, Katy's jaw drops. She watches in awe as Shaun fights off the others too. When an even bigger guy with a sword-forearm stands up, the people on the bus think Shaun has met his match. But Shaun beats this guy too. Katy is left with a question: Who on earth is he? "I know you don't like to talk about your life," she says, "but a guy with a freaking machete for an arm just chopped our bus in half!"[4]

4 *Shang-Chi and the Legend of the 10 Rings*, directed by Destin Daniel Cretton (Burbank, CA: Walt Disney Studios, 2021).

Matthew, Mark, and Luke each tell the story of a similarly disruptive moment for Jesus's friends. Jesus and his disciples are on a boat. It's evening. Tired from a day of teaching, Jesus falls asleep. But then a massive storm comes up. Waves are breaking into the boat and filling it. Several of Jesus's disciples were fishermen, and even they are terrified. But Jesus just sleeps on. They wake him up with, "Teacher, do you not care that we are perishing?" (Mark 4:38). What did they expect Jesus to do? Perhaps he'd be an extra pair of hands for bailing out? Or maybe he'd pray to God for the storm to start dying down? But Jesus, fresh from sleep, speaks to the wind and the sea: "Peace!" he says, "Be still!" (4:39). The wind stops, and there is a great calm. Then Jesus asks, "Why are you so afraid? Have you still no faith?" (4:40). We might expect the disciples to be relieved. "Phew! The storm is over. Jesus saved the day!" But they're not. Mark tells us they're "filled with great fear" and say to one another, "Who then is this that even the wind and the sea obey him?" (4:41).

In Genesis God spoke the oceans into being. In Exodus he drove the Red Sea back with a strong east wind and made a path so that his people could walk through on dry ground. Here, Jesus speaks to the wind and the sea, and they obey. This is no gradual calming of a storm. The brakes are crammed on suddenly, and his disciples are jolted from one fear to another. Like Katy, discovering that her friend Shaun is actually Shang-Chi, the son of the world's most powerful man, they're starting to see who Jesus is—and they are terrified.

Once again, Mark *is* telling us.

Why Do You Call Me Good?

In 1956, *The Chronicles of Narnia* author, C. S. Lewis, quietly married an American poet named Joy Davidman. Joy was raised Jewish and became an atheist and a Communist in early adulthood. But by the time she met Lewis, she'd turned to Christianity. After her chronically unfaithful husband, Bill, divorced her, Joy asked Lewis if he would marry her legally so that she could stay in England. He agreed. But a year later, Joy was diagnosed with cancer. Lewis (who went by "Jack" in private life) was devastated. In the film based on his life, he has this conversation with a fellow Oxford professor:

> HARRY. Well, she's your friend, of course, but, well. . . . She's not family.
>
> JACK. She's not my wife? Of course not. It's impossible. It's unthinkable. How could Joy have been my wife? I'd have to love her, wouldn't I? I'd have to care more for her than for anyone else in this world. I'd have to be suffering the torments of the damned at the prospect of losing her.
>
> HARRY. I'm sorry, Jack. I didn't know.
>
> JACK. Nor did I.

Jack tells his friend the truth about his love for Joy by saying it's impossible.[5]

One day a rich young man ran up to Jesus and knelt down to ask the most important question in the world: "Good Teacher, what must I do to inherit eternal life?" (Mark 10:17). Perhaps that question lingers in the back of your own mind. Not in those words. But if there *is* a God, you'd like to know how you could get in on eternal life. Jesus's first response is not an answer; it's a question: "Why do you call me good? No one is good except God alone" (10:18). In Jewish terms, it was impossible, unthinkable,

5 *Shadowlands*, directed by Richard Attenborough (Los Angeles: Paramont Pictures, 1993).

that Jesus could be God himself—the one eternal being, who is truly, deeply, unimaginably good. He'd have to do the things that only God could do.

Jesus then lists the six of the Ten Commandments that tell us how to treat each other: "You know the commandments: 'Do not murder, Do not commit adultery, Do not steal, Do not bear false witness, Do not defraud, Honor your father and mother'" (Mark 10:19). But he leaves out the first four, which tell us how to relate to God. The young man claims he's followed these six commandments since childhood. Jesus looks at him and loves him. "You lack one thing," he says. "Go, sell all that you have and give to the poor, and you will have treasure in heaven; and come, follow me" (10:21). To truly gain eternal life, this man must give up *everything* and follow Jesus. This is what following the first four God-oriented commandments looks like. But the young man finds the cost too high: "Disheartened by the saying, he went away sorrowful, for he had great possessions" (10:22).

This young man is confronted with what we'll all discover if we read the Gospels. Jesus doesn't want our spare time, our extra cash, our periodic prayers. He wants our everything. And only God can rightly ask for that. If Jesus isn't God himself, he isn't a good teacher. He's either a megalomaniac or a cold-hearted fraud, who claimed an identity to which he had no right. But if you read through any of the Gospels, you'll find there is no doubt he made the claim.

I Am . . .

Katy and Shaun are on a plane when she asks him who he is. Shaun explains that his name's not really Shaun, but Shang-Chi. After mispronouncing it a few times, Katy asks sarcastically, "You changed your name from Shang to Shaun? I wonder how your father found you!" It's not the greatest undercover alias. Shang-Chi was truly trying to conceal who he is—albeit incompetently. But when Jesus echoes the name of Israel's one true God, he's aiming for the opposite. He's taking the name of Israel's one true God and making it his own.

When Moses met with God speaking from a miraculously burning bush, God had called himself "I AM WHO I AM" (Ex. 3:14). In John's Gospel, Jesus plays with these words like a master composer exploring a motif:

- "I am the bread of life." (John 6:35, 48; cf. 6:41, 51)
- "I am the light of the world." (8:12)
- "I am the door of the sheep." (10:7; cf. 10:9)
- "I am the resurrection and the life." (11:25)
- "I am the good shepherd." (10:11, 14)
- "I am the way, and the truth, and the life." (14:6)
- "I am the true vine." (15:1; cf. 15:5)

Time and again, Jesus summons words and metaphors from Hebrew Scripture to present himself both as the true Israel and as Israel's one true God. We see two instances of this played out in one explosive conversation.

God's first words in the Bible are "Let there be light" (Gen. 1:3). Standing in the temple, Jesus declares, "I am the light of the world. Whoever follows me will not walk in darkness, but will have the light of life" (John 8:12). The boldness of this claim is breathtaking. Many religious leaders have claimed to be enlightened. But Jesus claims he *is* the light. What's more, we see the theme of light defeating darkness in the mouths of Israel's prophets. "The people who walked in darkness," Isaiah announced,

> have seen a great light;
> those who dwelt in a land of deep darkness,
> on them has light shone. (Isa. 9:2)

Isaiah ties these words to Galilee, where Jesus lived (Isa. 9:1). Matthew points to their fulfilment when Jesus moved there (Matt. 4:12–16), and adds an allusion to Psalm 23:4:

> For those dwelling in the region and shadow of death,
> on them a light has dawned. (Matt. 4:16)

Jesus is light and life breaking into darkness and death. Isaiah's prophecy goes on to speak of a God-given, everlasting King being born. His words must have rung in every Jewish ear when Jesus claimed to be the light of the world.

The Pharisees are not impressed. But Jesus doubles down. He tells them that they will die in their sins if they don't believe in him, but that if they live in his word, they will know the truth and the truth will set them free (John 8:24, 31–32). His hearers claim they're not enslaved to anyone. But Jesus argues that they're enslaved to sin, and he alone can set them free (8:31–38). Eventually, they ask, "Are you greater than our father Abraham who died? And the prophets died! Who do you make yourself out to be?" (8:53). Jesus replies, "Your father Abraham rejoiced that he would see my day. He saw it and was glad" (8:56). Now they know Jesus is crazy. "You are not yet fifty years old," they object, "and have you seen Abraham?" (8:57). Then Jesus delivers his final blow: "Truly, truly, I say to you, before Abraham was, I am" (8:58). The Jewish leaders knew precisely what he meant. His claim to be the great "I am" was blasphemy. "They picked up stones to throw at him" (8:59).

What about One God?

In some ways, the reaction of the Jewish leaders was understandable. God's oneness was the heartbeat of their faith. "Hear, O Israel: The LORD our God, the LORD is one," Moses had proclaimed. "You shall love the LORD your God with all your heart and with all your soul and with all your might" (Deut. 6:4–5). In a world that venerated many gods, the Jews believed in one Creator God who stood alone and who alone was worthy of their worship. Jesus says this is the greatest commandment of all (Matt. 22:27). But in another confrontation in the temple, Jesus declares, "I and the Father are one" (John 10:30). Yes, there is one God, Jesus affirms. There's only one true Maker of all things. But Jesus claims he *is* that God.

We cannot fully wrap our minds around this. During the Tokyo Olympics, my kids were mesmerized by synchronized diving. Two people train for years until they can fly through the air precisely in sync. The world's best divers are almost perfectly aligned as they contort and turn and slice into the water. But they're still two bodies tumbling down. They attempt to think as one. But they're not one. The Jews were told, "The LORD our God, the LORD is one," and Jesus claims he's one with that same Lord. Once again, Jesus's hearers pick up stones to throw at him (John 10:31). Once again, he gets away. But it was only a question of time before his teachings got him killed. And that was not a tragic accident. It was the plan.

The Way, the Truth, the Life

The Doctor first met Amy Pond when she was seven. He crash-landed his time-and-space-ship, the TARDIS (short for "Time

And Relative Dimension In Space"), outside the front door of her house and ate with her. Then he said he needed to test drive his TARDIS, but he'd come back for her in five minutes. Amy packed her bags and waited. But he didn't come. In fact, she was nineteen when they met again. But when he did come back, he showed her all the universe and utterly transformed her life.

On the night that Jesus was arrested, he told his disciples that he was about to leave them so that he might prepare a place for them in his Father's house. He said he'd come back and take them to be with him: "You know the way to where I am going," Jesus added (John 14:4). One of his disciples, Thomas, asked, "Lord, we don't know where you are going. How can we know the way?" (14:5). Jesus replied with these breathtaking words: "I am the way, and the truth, and the life. No one comes to the Father except through me. If you had known me, you would have known my Father also. From now on, you do know him and have seen him" (14:6–7).

This famous "I am" statement builds on itself. Jesus is the way to get to God. But he's not just the path. He's the destination too. Many religious leaders have claimed to teach truth. But Jesus says he *is* the truth. Many have claimed to give guidance for life. But Jesus claims he *is* the life. Apart from him is only death. To know him is to know the Father too.

Another disciple, Philip, replies, "Lord, show us the Father, and it is enough for us." But Jesus asks, "Have I been with you so long, and you still do not know me, Philip?" (14:8–9). Meeting Jesus is even more exciting than meeting someone who can travel time and space. It means meeting God himself: the one who made the universe, and time and space, and everything we've ever loved or dreamed of. It means the world—and it means heaven too. But is it just the stuff of fairytales and sci-fi fantasy?

Doubting Thomas

If you find it hard to believe that Jesus is indeed the Son of God, you're in good company. Jesus's Jewish disciples believed there was one true Creator God. But after years of traveling with Jesus, they were only just beginning to grasp who he is. And then the unthinkable happened: Jesus died on a Roman cross. The crucifixion should have been the final proof that Jesus *wasn't* God: the proof that he could not oppose the power of Rome, the proof that he was not the great "I AM." And if Jesus had stayed dead, that proof would have been undeniable. But all four Gospels claim that Jesus pulled a jailbreak from death. The Son of God, they claim, defeated death itself. But one of Jesus's disciples refused to believe.

When Jesus first appeared to his disciples after his resurrection, Thomas wasn't there. The others told him, "We have seen the Lord!" But Thomas replied, "Unless I see in his hands the mark of the nails, and place my finger into the mark of the nails, and place my hand into his side, I will never believe" (John 20:25). All Thomas's hopes had been crushed by Jesus's death, and he wasn't fool enough to have them raised again. Perhaps you feel a little bit like this. Perhaps you thought there was a God when you were growing up. Perhaps you prayed. Perhaps you hoped there might be truth in all of this, but now you've lived through painful things, and it just feels so unbelievable. Perhaps you think, like Thomas, you'd believe it if you saw it. If so, the end of Thomas's story is for you. Eight days later, Jesus came again, and Thomas was there. Exposing his own crucifixion scars, Jesus said to Thomas, "Put your finger here, and see my hands; and put out your hand, and place it in my side. Do not disbelieve, but believe." Thomas responded with the only conclusion he could draw from the evidence before him: "My Lord and my God!" (20:27–28).

So What?

What does it mean for us that the Creator God became a man in Jesus Christ? It means that you and I are fully and completely known. It means we're known more fully than a mother knows her baby, than an artist knows his paintings, than a novelist knows her imaginary world. It means the one who made us lived and died, hungered and thirsted, sweat and bled for love of us. It means the one who made the stars has wept for us. It means the one who stretched out space stretched out his arms and died for us. River doesn't tell the Doctor she is Amy's baby. She shows him. She turns defeat to victory by showing up and showing who she is. If Jesus is the everlasting Son of God, it means defeat is turned to victory for anyone who follows him. It means the God who made the universe has come at last for you and me. It means the world turned upside down—for us.

3

Jesus the King

THE CLASSIC FILM *Gladiator* is set in AD 180. In the opening scene, a Roman general, Maximus, leads his legionaries to victory over Germanic tribes. On his return, the emperor, Marcus Aurelius, asks Maximus to step in when he dies and make Rome a republic once again. But when the emperor's son, Commodus, hears of this plan, he murders his father, proclaims himself emperor, and demands Maximus's allegiance. Maximus refuses, escapes Commodus's men, and heads for home. He's been counting the days until he sees his wife and son again. But when he gets back home at last, he finds they've been crucified by Commodus's troops.

Exhausted and despairing, Maximus collapses. He's picked up by slave traders, who sell him as a gladiator. In a pivotal scene, we watch this man who has lost everything win victory before the emperor himself. When Commodus enters the arena and asks his name, Maximus pulls off his helmet and declares, "My name is Maximus Decimus Meridius, commander of the Armies of the North, General of the Felix Legions and loyal servant to the *true* emperor, Marcus Aurelius. Father to a murdered son. Husband to a murdered wife. And I will have my vengeance, in this life or the next."[1]

The Jews of Jesus's day were waiting for a hero who would overthrow the Romans and establish Israel once again. They had returned from exile in Babylon. But foreigners still ruled them, and through the prophets, God had promised them an empire-conquering King. In this chapter, we'll see how the Gospels shine a light on Jesus as this King, but how his victory inverted what his fellow countrymen expected—and why we twenty-first-century folk should still yearn for God's everlasting King.

Jesus Christ, the Son of God

When Commodus first asks Maximus, "Why doesn't the hero reveal himself, and tell us all your *real* name?" Maximus replies, "My name is Gladiator." Commodus objects. That's not his name; it's his role. Likewise, when Jesus is called *Christ*, it's not his name. The Hebrew word *Messiah* means "anointed one" and sprang from the ancient practice by which the kings of Israel were set apart by having oil smeared on their heads. The word *Christ* comes from the Greek translation of *Messiah.* For centuries, prophets sent by God had promised an empire-breaking, Israel-saving, death-defying, everlasting King. Just as Maximus was not just *a* gladiator but the ultimate Gladiator, the Gospel authors claim that Jesus is not just *a* king, but *the* King.

Mark's Gospel opens with this claim: "The beginning of the gospel of Jesus Christ, the Son of God" (Mark 1:1). To us, "the Son of God" sounds first and foremost like a claim to Jesus's divinity. As we saw in chapter 2, Jesus did claim to be God's

1 *Gladiator*, directed by Ridley Scott (Universal City: CA: DreamWorks Pictures, 2000).

everlasting Son—who with the Father and the Spirit is the one true God. But Jews of Jesus's day would have heard *Son of God* primarily as meaning "Christ." Just as *commander in chief* means "president" to Americans, so *Son of God* communicated "Christ." Matthew fronts the claim as well: "The book of the genealogy of Jesus Christ, the son of David, the son of Abraham" (Matt. 1:1). David was Israel's archetypal king, and Matthew retells Israel's history through a genealogy that goes from Abraham (the father of the faith) to David (the greatest king) to the exile in Babylon (the epic disaster) to the coming of Jesus "who is called Christ" (1:16).

Like a general directing his archers, Luke takes a more "wait for it" approach. But when the arrows fly, they come in style. An angel appears to Mary to tell her she'll give birth to a son. "He will be great and will be called the Son of the Most High," the angel explains. "And the Lord God will give to him the throne of his father David, and he will reign over the house of Jacob forever, and of his kingdom there will be no end" (Luke 1:32–33).

For Jews of Jesus's day living under Roman rule, the coming of God's long-awaited King meant everything. But for most of us today, the idea of Jesus as King may feel like a delivery we didn't order. We might enjoy watching *The Crown* on Netflix, but none of us longs for a return to royal rule. We know from the grinding of history that when one person is in charge—whether a monarch or a supreme leader under another name—we'll likely have a tyrant before long. Even systems like communism that supposedly exalt equality can quickly slump into dictatorship. So, we have forged democracies to try and spread the power out. It's not a perfect system, but we stick with it and hope for the best. As Winston Churchill quipped, "Democracy is the worst form of Government except for all those other forms that have been tried from time to time."[2] So how can we make sense of Jesus's claim to be the King today?

Ironically, the very thing that would have dashed the hopes of Jesus's contemporaries is what should give us hope in Jesus as God's everlasting King today. According to the expectations of his fellow countrymen, Jesus's attempt to claim the kingship was a failure. Instead of taking up the throne, Jesus had taken up a cross. Instead of taking power for himself, he'd given it all up. Instead of beating others down in conquest, he'd lifted up the most despised in his society with tender care. Instead of the cross being his moment of defeat, it represents his greatest victory. By suffering injustice, Jesus came to roll out justice like the world has never seen before.

Good News

When Maximus defeated the Germanic tribes, the emperor, Marcus Aurelius, might have issued a *euangelion*—a proclamation of the good news. In English, this Greek word is translated by a word that has come to carry massive spiritual weight: *gospel.* When we hear that word, we might think of the four Gospels of Matthew, Mark, Luke, and John; or of the basic gospel message of the Christian faith; or perhaps of gospel music sung by artists like Aretha Franklin. But for the people who first heard the word on Jesus's lips, *euangelion* would have carried political weight. To be sure, for Jews, there was spiritual weight too. "How beautiful upon the mountains," declared Isaiah,

2 From a speech in the House of Commons on November 11, 1947. See *Irrepressible Churchill: A Treasury of Winston Churchill's Wit,* selected and compiled by Kay Halle (Cleveland, OH: World, 1966), 279.

> are the feet of him who brings good news,
> who publishes peace, who brings good news of happiness,
> who publishes salvation,
> who says to Zion, "Your God reigns." (Isa. 52:7)

Isaiah was first written in Hebrew, but in early Greek translations, the verb for "bring good news" was *euangelizō*. The corresponding noun for "good news / gospel" is *euangelion*. But even here, the good news or gospel is about a coming king. All of this is channeled in Jesus's first recorded sermon in Mark: "The time is fulfilled, and the kingdom of God is at hand; repent and believe in the gospel" (Mark 1:15). These words are dangerous: a challenge to the power of Rome and a call to submit to the incoming God-ordained King. But what would this King be like?

Jesus's first recorded sermon in Luke answers this question. It's delivered in his hometown synagogue in Nazareth. Jesus is handed the scroll of the prophet Isaiah. He finds the passage he wants, and he reads,

> The Spirit of the Lord is upon me,
> Because he has anointed me
> to proclaim good news to the poor.
> He has sent me to proclaim liberty to the captives
> and recovering of sight to the blind,
> to set at liberty those who are oppressed,
> to proclaim the year of the Lord's favor. (Luke 4:18–19)

Then Jesus rolls up the scroll, gives it back to the attendant, and sits down. Everyone's eyes are fixed on him. "Today," he says, "this Scripture has been fulfilled in your hearing" (4:21).

My guess is that for most of us, this manifesto of Jesus's kingship sounds attractive. We'd like to live in a society marked by justice, compassion, liberty, and healing. But we don't feel a desperate craving in our bones for rescue. While we may care about liberty and justice for all, we're likely not dying without it for ourselves. But just as the Allies' victory was desperately good news for the surviving Jews in Nazi concentration camps and for the Londoners beleaguered by the Blitz, so Jesus being God's anointed King is good news for the suffering and oppressed. He's come to elevate the destitute. He's come to liberate the prisoners. He's come to give sight to the physically and spiritually blind. He's come for those who feel their desperate need of him. This is the kind of King that Jesus is, and his prison-breaking kingdom is still rolling out today—whether we realize it or not.

The claim that "the arc of the moral universe is long, but it bends toward justice" has become a mantra of secular humanism. Many who don't believe in God nevertheless believe there is a right and a wrong side of history, and the progression of history—albeit slow—is naturally toward justice. One of the great progressions people tend to cite to prove this is the success of the Civil Rights Movement. Indeed, many know the quote about the arc of the moral universe being long because it was invoked by the Rev. Dr. Martin Luther King Jr. But few remember how King used that quote. In 1958, in a piece titled "Out of the Long Night of Segregation," he proclaimed, "Evil may so shape events that Caesar will occupy a palace and Christ a cross, but that same Christ will rise up and split history into A.D. and B.C., so that even the life of Caesar must be dated by his name. Yes, 'the arc of the moral universe is long, but it bends toward justice.'"[3]

3 Quoted from James H. Washington, ed., *A Testament of Hope: The Essential Writings and Speeches of Martin Luther King Jr* (New York: HarperOne, 2003), 9.

King's confidence was not derived from some impersonal force. It depended on his faith in Jesus's everlasting, empire-quelling rule.

Martin Luther King was clearly a religious guy, but can't we just have justice without Jesus? No. If we rip this central pillar out, we have no reason to believe there is a moral arc to the universe at all—let alone that it will bend toward justice. Israeli historian Yuval Noah Harari gives us a clear-sighted, atheist perspective in his global bestseller, *Sapiens: A Brief History of Humankind*, when he declares, "There are no gods in the universe, no nations, no money, no human rights, no laws, and no justice outside the common imagination of human beings."[4] Commenting on the Declaration of Independence, Harari notes that "[t]heAmericans got the idea of equality from Christianity," and he calls human rights "figments of our fertile imaginations."[5] Another famous atheist, Richard Dawkins, observes that "moral values are 'in the air' and they change from century to century, even from decade to decade."[6] In fact, as we'll see in chapter 5, when we look back at history, we'll find that the very standards by which we judge the moral universe today were given to us (whether we realize it or not) by Jesus the Christ: the King who wore his crown upon the cross. But Jesus didn't come to bring justice and healing only between human beings. He also came to bring justice and healing between us human beings and the holy, perfect, righteous God who made us.

When Jesus rolled up the scroll and sat down in that synagogue two thousand years ago, he claimed he was anointed by God to put things right. But what he didn't read would have been as striking to

4 Yuval Noah Harari, *Sapiens: A Brief History of Humankind* (New York: Harper, 2015), 28.

5 Harari, *Sapiens*, 108, 32.

6 Richard Dawkins, *Outgrowing God: A Beginners Guide* (New York: Random House, 2019), 159.

his hearers as what he did. In Isaiah, the words after which Jesus rolls up the scroll—"to proclaim the year of the Lord's favor"—form the first half of a thought which ends, "and the day of vengeance of our God" (Isa. 61:2). Jesus stopped mid-sentence. The time of opportunity is now: the year of the Lord's favor, when rebels could surrender and come home. Judgment day is still to come, when each of us will give an account to our Maker for our sin, when none of us will have a chance to stand up on our own account. But as of now, it's not too late to turn around and throw ourselves upon the mercy of the Judge.

Last summer I wept as I read to my kids the moment in *Harry Potter and the Deathly Hallows* when Percy Weasley shows up. He's been a fool, aligning with the Ministry of Magic that's being controlled by Lord Voldemort. But unexpectedly, at last, he comes to fight with his family and friends against Voldemort's army.[7] It's not too late for him to change his mind. And as we see throughout the Gospels, it's not too late for us to turn around and put our trust in Jesus who alone can carry the weight of our sin.

You might expect the Jews of Nazareth to dance in the streets at Jesus's message. Not only was God's kingdom on its way, but one of their own local boys was God's anointed King! When Sunisa Lee won an Olympic gold in gymnastics, her hometown in Minnesota organized a parade. How much more should Nazareth have celebrated their homegrown Messiah! At first they all speak well of him and marvel at his words (Luke 4:22). But soon the mood in the room turns. Against their patriotic expectations, Jesus highlights God's care for those *outside* of Israel (4:25–27). His hearers are so furious that they try to throw him off a cliff.

7 J. K. Rowling, *Harry Potter and the Deathly Hallows* (New York: Scolastic, 2009), 605.

You could say that this wasn't a great start to Jesus's preaching ministry. But it was the trajectory he chose from the first. The arc of Jesus's life was bending toward the cross. But even his closest disciples couldn't understand.

Who Do You Say That I Am?

Our social media culture has forced us to get pithy. On Instagram you have 150 characters to summarize your bio. On Twitter it's a generous 160. The really famous people go for less. Simone Biles writes, "Olympic Gold Medalist. Dog Mom. Pizza connoisseur." Taylor Swift describes herself as: "Happy, free, confused and lonely at the same time."[8] We know who she is. But when the most famous man in all of history asked his followers who people thought he was, he got a mixed response.

At a pivotal moment in Matthew's Gospel, Jesus asks his followers, "Who do people say that the Son of Man is?" (Matt. 16:13). They answer, "Some say John the Baptist, others say Elijah, and others Jeremiah or one of the prophets" (16:14). Then Jesus follows up, "But who do you say that I am?" (16:15). Simon Peter replies, "You are the Christ, the Son of the living God" (16:16). At first, Jesus strongly affirms Simon Peter: "Blessed are you, Simon Bar-Jonah! For flesh and blood has not revealed this to you, but my Father who is in heaven. And I tell you, you are Peter, and on this rock I will build my church, and the gates of hell shall not prevail against it" (16:17–18). The name Peter meant "rock." How Peter's heart must have swelled at these words! But then, disappointingly, Jesus "strictly charged the disciples to tell no one that he was the Christ" (16:20).

8 Simone Biles (@simonebiles) and Taylor Swift (@taylorswift), Instagram, https://www.instagram.com, accessed October 19, 2021.

Perhaps at this point the disciples think that Jesus is going to be like those presidential candidates who *definitely aren't going to run* until they do. Maybe he's just biding his time, getting the right endorsements lined up. But things get worse. "From that time," Matthew tells us, "Jesus began to show his disciples that he must go to Jerusalem and suffer many things from the elders and chief priests and scribes, and be killed, and on the third day be raised" (Matt. 16:21). Far from gaining the right endorsements and rising to power, Jesus says he's going to *fail* to get endorsements from the powers that be. In fact, he'll end up nailed to a cross—like all the other failed messiahs.

Peter won't hear of it. As newly minted chief of staff, he takes Jesus aside and says, "Far be it from you, Lord! This shall never happen to you!" (16:22). But Jesus turns to him and says, "Get behind me, Satan! You are a hindrance to me. For you are not setting your mind on the things of God, but on the things of man" (16:23). How those words must have stung. Peter was all geared up to be Jesus's right-hand man. Perhaps he felt vice-presidential vibes. But here is Jesus calling him Satan! Then things get even worse. Turning to his disciples, Jesus says, "If anyone would come after me, let him deny himself and take up his cross and follow me. For whoever would save his life will lose it, but whoever loses his life for my sake will find it. For what will it profit a man if he gains the whole world and forfeits his soul?" (16:24–26). Jesus isn't just risking crucifixion by his claim to be the Christ. He's planning on it. What's more, he says that all his followers are called to give their lives up too.

Perhaps you can think of a time when you've been willing to give up everything for what you wanted most. A relationship. A job. An image of yourself that you were desperate to project. In Oscar

Wilde's *The Picture of Dorian Gray*, the central character gazes at his portrait and says,

> How sad it is! I shall grow old, and horrible, and dreadful. But this picture will remain always young. . . . If it were only the other way! If it were I who was to be always young, and the picture that was to grow old! For that—for that—I would give everything! Yes, there is nothing in the whole world I would not give! I would give my soul for that![9]

As the book progresses, we find that Dorian's wish came true. He's clung onto youth and beauty while this picture in his attic has aged and taken on the features of his selfishness and cruelty. At one point, his mentor, Lord Henry, asks him casually, "'What does it profit a man if he gain the whole world and lose'—how does the quotation run?—'his own soul'?" He'd heard "some vulgar street-preacher" in London quote these words of Jesus, and he brought the question back to Dorian. "Don't, Harry," Dorian replies, "The soul is a terrible reality. It can be bought, and sold, and bartered away."[10] Dorian got what he thought he wanted and lost the only thing that mattered in the end. But Jesus is willing to give up every earthly good—even to die an early, agonizing death on a cross—to gain a heavenly kingdom. The point was not for him to have power and glory. He had those things already from all eternity. The point was us.

Like Dorian's picture, Jesus took our sin upon himself. But rather than ruining our souls in exchange, he wraps us in his warm embrace. If we give up everything to follow him, he'll keep our souls

9 Oscar Wilde, *The Picture of Dorian Gray* (London: Penguin Classics, 2003), 205.

10 Wilde, *The Picture of Dorian Gray*, 205.

and bodies safe in his strong arms. He is the King who's come to rescue us, and unlike any other king, he knows us individually. In fact, he seeks us out.

The Woman at the Well

In the first chapter of John's Gospel, multiple characters point to Jesus's identity as the Christ. First, John the Baptist clarifies that he himself is not the Christ but that he's come to prepare the way. He says of Jesus, "I have seen and borne witness that this is the Son of God" (John 1:34). Then one of John's disciples, Andrew, starts following Jesus and tells his brother, Simon Peter, "'We have found the Messiah' (which means Christ)" (1:41). Then Nathanael—who famously asked if anything good could come from Nazareth—meets Jesus and declares, "Rabbi, you are the Son of God! You are the King of Israel!" (1:49). But it's not until later in John's Gospel that Jesus himself first explicitly identifies himself as the Christ. And when he does, he shares this stunning news with a most unlikely person.

Jesus's disciples have left him to find food. He's sitting by a well, and he asks a Samaritan woman for a drink. She's taken aback: "How is it that you, a Jew, ask for a drink from me, a woman of Samaria?" (4:9). The Jews of Jesus's day despised Samaritans. They'd travel long distances to avoid Samaritan land. Drinking with a Samaritan would have compromised Jesus's reputation by itself. The fact that she's a woman makes it even more problematic. As their conversation unfolds, we find the situation is even worse: this woman has had five husbands, and the man she is now living with is not her husband. In Jewish terms, she's literally the last person Jesus should be seen with. But Jesus isn't taken aback. He knew exactly who she was when he asked her for a drink.

The Samaritan woman can see that Jesus is a prophet, so she starts asking him theological questions. In their last exchange, she says, "I know that Messiah is coming (he who is called Christ). When he comes, he will tell us all things." Jesus replies, "I who speak to you am he." (4:25–26). At this mic-drop moment, Jesus's disciples return. They're stunned to find he's talking with this woman. But she leaves her water jar and goes back to her town. This woman is so overwhelmed by Jesus that she ditches her means of gathering water and says to everyone she meets, "Come, see a man who told me all that I ever did. Can this be the Christ?" (4:28–29).

Jesus is the kind of King who wastes his time with people others would despise. In fact, this is his longest recorded private conversation in any of the Gospels. He knows exactly who this woman is, and she becomes a missionary to her town. Many come to see Jesus and believe in him because of her simple testimony: "He told me all that I ever did" (4:39). Jesus's intimate, supernatural knowledge of this woman authenticates his claim to be the Christ. I sometimes worry that if people really knew me, they'd realize I'm not lovable: like an unwrapped chocolate bar that turns out to be tasteless, or worse. Perhaps you feel that way sometimes too. But Jesus knows us inside out, and still he reaches out to us in love. Jesus's kingship is personal. But it's also universal. After hearing from Jesus for themselves, the other Samaritans say to the woman, "It is no longer because of what you said that we believe, for we have heard for ourselves, and we know that this is indeed the Savior of the world" (4:42).

Hosanna to the Son of David

In *Gladiator*, Maximus at first conceals his identity. It's not yet time for Commodus to realize who he is. Likewise, time and again in the Gospels, Jesus tells people to keep quiet about his claim to be the

Christ. But then the day comes for the news to hit the streets. Jesus is getting ready to go up to Jerusalem, and he sends his disciples to borrow a donkey. This seems like a strange mode of transport for God's long-awaited King: like driving a minivan into town instead of a Mercedes. But that's the point. Matthew connects this moment to a prophecy from Zechariah:

> Say to the daughter of Zion,
> "Behold, your king is coming to you,
> humble, and mounted on a donkey,
> on a colt, the foal of a beast of burden." (Matt. 21:4–5)

Even as he rides into Jerusalem as King, Jesus comes humbly. But the Jews of Jerusalem get it. They spread cloaks and palm branches on the road: the ancient Jewish equivalent of rolling out a red carpet. It's a dangerous scene.

In *Gladiator*, when Maximus at last reveals who he is, the emperor's guards turn their swords on him. But the crowd in the arena forces Commodus to give the thumbs up sign by shouting, "Live! Live! Live! Live!" Similarly, when Jesus finally makes a public claim to kingship, the crowds in Jerusalem are shouting the equivalent of "King! King! King! King!" "Hosanna to the Son of David!" they cry. "Blessed is he who comes in the name of the Lord!" (Matt. 21:9). "Hosanna" means "[God,] save, please," and the "Son of David" marks Jesus out as the Christ: the heir of Israel's greatest king. Jesus's disciples shout as well: "Blessed is the King who comes in the name of the Lord!" (Luke 19:38). The Pharisees are horrified: "Teacher," they demand, "rebuke your disciples." But Jesus replies with one of my favorite lines in all the Gospels: "I tell you, if these were silent, the very stones would cry out" (19:39–40).

Jesus doesn't need the crowds to validate his kingship. The gravel on the ground is ready to declare it at this point. The one who made the universe has come to claim his kingdom here on earth, and if the people that he made can't see what's happening, the stones will shout it out. Like Maximus, Jesus survived that day. But as with Maximus, it's only a matter of time: these cloaks and shouts and palm branches are marking out his way not just to coronation but to death.

The King of the Jews

If anyone should have welcomed the Messiah, it was the chief priests and the elders. But instead, they have Jesus arrested. At his trial, the high priest demands, "I adjure you by the living God, tell us if you are the Christ, the Son of God." Jesus replies, "You have said so. But I tell you, from now on you will see the Son of Man seated at the right hand of Power and coming on the clouds of heaven" (Matt. 26:63–64). They know what Jesus means by this. The "Son of Man" was Jesus's favorite way of referring to himself. It tied in with a vision in the book of Daniel, where Daniel declares,

> I saw in the night visions,
>
> and behold, with the clouds of heaven
> there came one like a son of man,
> and he came to the Ancient of Days
> and was presented before him.
> And to him was given dominion
> and glory and a kingdom
> that all peoples, nations, and languages
> should serve him;
> his dominion is an everlasting dominion,

which shall not pass away,
and his kingdom one
that shall not be destroyed. (Dan. 7:13–14)

When Jesus tells the high priest he'll see the Son of Man coming on the clouds of heaven, he's claiming to be God's eternal, universal King. The high priest tears his robes in horror, saying, "He has uttered blasphemy. What further witnesses do we need? You have now heard his blasphemy. What is your judgment?" The other leaders answer, "He deserves death." Then they spit in his face and slap him, saying, "Prophesy to us, you Christ! Who is it that struck you?" (Matt. 26:65–68).

Rather than stoning him themselves, the chief priests send Jesus to the Roman governor, Pilate, who asks him, "Are you the King of the Jews?" Jesus answers, "You have said so," and refuses to defend himself (Matt. 27:11–14). Pilate's impressed. There was a tradition that at the Passover the governor would release one prisoner to the Jews who had gathered in Jerusalem to celebrate, so Pilate asks the people if they want Jesus released. Like the crowd in the arena shouting to save Maximus's life, the crowds in Jerusalem could have called for Jesus's release. But the chief priests and elders persuade them to do the opposite. They call instead for the release of a notorious prisoner, Barabbas. When Pilate asks, "Then what shall I do with Jesus who is called Christ?" they say, "Let him be crucified!" Pilate responds, "Why? What evil has he done?" But they shout all the more, "Let him be crucified!" (27:22–23). So Pilate had Jesus whipped and handed him over to be crucified.

The Roman soldiers had a bit of fun. They stripped Jesus naked, dressed him in a scarlet robe, and rammed a crown of thorns onto his head. Then they put a staff in his right hand like a fake scepter and knelt down, saying, "Hail, King of the Jews!" They spat on him and hit him with the scepter-stick before leading him away to his excruciating death (27:28–31). On the cross above his head, they pinned the charge against him: "This is Jesus, the King of the Jews" (27:37). The accusation was completely accurate. But crucifixion wasn't the stamp of failure on Jesus the King. It was the arena where he won his victory.

Jesus, Remember Me When You Come into Your Kingdom

As people heckled Jesus on the cross, the irony became yet more pronounced. The Jewish leaders mocked him, saying, "He saved others; let him save himself, if he is the Christ of God, his Chosen One!" (Luke 23:35). The Romans mocked him too: "If you are the King of the Jews, save yourself!" (23:37). Even one of the two criminals crucified with Jesus hurled insults, saying, "Are you not the Christ? Save yourself and us!" (23:39). *Save yourself. Save yourself. Save yourself. If you're so powerful, Jesus, save yourself,* they said. But Jesus hadn't come to save himself. He'd come to save us.

The criminal hanging on one side of Jesus responded to the criminal on the other side, "Do you not fear God, since you are under the same sentence of condemnation? And we indeed justly, for we are receiving the due reward of our deeds; but this man has done nothing wrong" (23:40–41). And then he turned to Jesus and said these unbelievable words: "Jesus, remember me when you come into your kingdom" (23:42). Death on a cross was the sign of a failed messiah. But this criminal, in the last agonizing moments of his life, sees who Jesus really is. Like the woman at the well, he's the last kind of person Jesus should have welcomed. But he does: "Truly, I say to you," Jesus replied, "today you will be with me in paradise" (23:43).

As we saw in chapter 1, the four Gospels were written down decades after Jesus's death. And yet from the first they declare that he is King. His crucifixion wasn't where he failed. It was the step he took up to his throne. He hadn't come to overthrow the Romans. He'd come to conquer sin and death by taking them upon himself. This doesn't make the slightest shred of sense if Jesus wasn't raised to life again. We'll come to that in chapter 9. But if he did come back to everlasting life, it means that he is the King who conquered death itself and that his victory message—his *euangelion*—is still ringing out.

So What?

What difference does it make to us if Jesus is God's death-defying, never-ending, empire-breaking King? What difference does it make if he's good news for the imprisoned, blind, poor, and oppressed—for prostitutes, for outcasts, for five-time divorcees, for even hardened criminals? It means that one day, all that's wrong will be put right. It means that any power today will one day be torn down when Jesus comes back to rule forevermore. It means we must switch sides and put our trust in Jesus now, before it is too late. But if we do, we can be part of Jesus's justice-bringing, prison-breaking, poor-protecting kingdom even now, and we can drink the living water of eternal life with him forevermore. When Maximus revealed who he was in the arena, he promised Commodus that he would have his vengeance, in this life or the next. If we are Jesus's people, we must fight with Jesus's weapon of self-sacrificing, power-flipping, unrelenting love. Because Jesus will bring justice—in this life and the next.

4

Jesus the Healer

AS I WRITE THIS, I've just returned home from having three lumps biopsied. The doctor told me there's a 50 percent chance they're cancerous. In cancer terms, I'm young. But a friend of mine six years younger was recently diagnosed with advanced breast cancer. Age is no guarantee. As I write these words, I don't know if I'm fine or very sick. I don't know if I'm facing surgeries or chemotherapy or worse. I don't know if I'll have to tell my kids their mummy has cancer. Because I believe what the Gospels say, I deeply believe that Jesus has the power to heal. But I don't know if he will.

In this chapter, we'll trace the therapeutic thread that weaves its way right through Jesus's life—from his first miracles, like the healing of Peter's feverish mother-in-law (Mark 1:30–31), to the night of his arrest, when he healed the high priest's servant, whose ear Peter had cut off (Luke 22:50–51; John 18:10). We'll see that Jesus has the power to heal both physical and spiritual wounds. But his ultimate promise is not of physical healing here and now, but resurrection life forevermore.

It's Not the Healthy Who Need a Doctor

My first routine mammogram revealed the lumps I had biopsied. The horror of cancer is how quietly it sneaks up, encroaching on us unawares, until we're very sick—or even dying. So we've found ways to see under the skin and catch cancer spinning its webs before we're so entangled that we can't get free. To have a hope of getting well, we need to know we're sick.

Right after they narrate the story of Jesus both healing and forgiving the paralyzed man (which we explored in chapter 2), Matthew, Mark, and Luke tell us that Jesus called a tax collector. This was like recruiting from the opposition. Faithful Jews saw tax collectors as anti-patriotic sinners. Instead of resisting Roman rule, they partnered with the Romans to extort taxes from their own people—and to fill their own pockets. But when Jesus tells this tax collector, "Follow me," he gets up right away (Luke 5:27–28). What's more, he throws a party for his newfound Lord. The Pharisees are scandalized. They ask Jesus's disciples, "Why do you eat and drink with tax collectors and sinners?" (5:30). Jesus replies, "Those who are well have no need of a physician, but those who are sick. I have not come to call the righteous but sinners to repentance" (5:31–32).

Jesus doesn't disagree with the Pharisees' diagnosis. He doesn't say the tax collectors are good guys really, who've just been led astray a bit. No. They're desperately spiritually sick. But Jesus's words are dangerous. The Pharisees can't see how sick they are, and so they're stuck—looking in on the party from the outside—while the sinful tax collectors know they need a doctor. Mark and Luke call this tax collector Levi (Mark 2:14; Luke 5:27). But Matthew calls him Matthew (Matt. 9:9). An early tradition associates Matthew's Gospel with this tax collector. If this is accurate, the most gloriously Jewish of all the Gospels preserves for us the testimony of a man rejected by the religious leaders of his day, who knew he needed a spiritual doctor. "Truly, I say to you," Jesus later warns the chief priests and elders, "the tax collectors and the prostitutes go into the kingdom of God before you" (Matt. 21:31).

My guess is most of us are more afraid of physical sickness than some nebulous spiritual kind. Right now, as I await my diagnosis, it's tempting to feel like the most important question is, "Do I have cancer?" But if Jesus is the Son of God, it's not. Our most important sickness is spiritual. We're all terminally ill. Without a doctor sent by God himself, there is no hope. Conversely, if our bodies are wasting away, but we're held in Jesus's arms, we're fundamentally well. I recently had dinner with an older friend with stage 4 cancer. She said she hasn't prayed for healing once. She's not afraid to die. In fact, she's praying, "Lord, take me home." She's ready for his ultimate embrace. So does Jesus care at all about our bodies? Yes.

I Will

In March 2021, I tested positive for COVID-19. At once I had to quarantine. I couldn't see my friends or hug my kids or hold my husband's hand. All human touch was stripped away—for a few days. One of the first people Jesus heals in Mark had likely lived like this for years. One day a leper kneels in front of Jesus, saying, "If you will, you can make me clean" (Mark 1:40). Leprosy was thought to be highly contagious. Lepers were required to live away from other people, for fear of spreading their flesh-festering disease. It was a social death sentence. We know from other Gospel accounts that Jesus could heal people from a distance. He just had to say the word. But when this leper kneels before him, Jesus, "moved with pity," stretches out his hand and touches him. "I will," he says. "Be clean" (1:41).

At this one loving touch from Jesus's hand, the leper's rotting and disfigured flesh reformed itself. Far from his death-bringing sickness spreading to Jesus, Jesus's life-giving wellness spread to him. Today, we've learned to treat leprosy with six to twelve months of drug therapy. But on that day, Jesus treated leprosy with one loving touch. Jesus told his patient to keep quiet about what had happened, but the ex-leper couldn't help himself. He went out and began to spread the news, faster than he could ever have spread his disease (Mark 1:45). Jesus didn't heal this man for show. He healed him because he cared. But Jesus doesn't always heal the ones he loves—at least, not yet.

One day last month, I came downstairs and saw the milk I use for my morning latte left out on the sideboard. I was so annoyed. I knew my milk was running low and almost out of date. But I'd also assured myself the night before that there was just enough for one more day. My husband, I assumed, had used my milk up on his cereal and now there was barely a dribble left. How inconsiderate! There was other milk he could have used, but he had selfishly drained mine. I stalked to the fridge to get the other milk. But when I opened the fridge door, I found a full, fresh carton of my milk. I realized in that moment that my husband hadn't used my old milk up. He'd stopped on his way home from work to buy me more because he'd seen that I was running low. Sometimes, we feel so angry with God for letting our bodies get sick. We know that he could heal us if he wanted. We know he could eke out the health we have for one more day. But in the end, his promise is of resurrection life: a whole new fresh and unexpiring body, designed to live with him forevermore. But we must put our trust in him and let the old, expiring body go. So, does this promise of a resurrection body mean we shouldn't pray for healing now? No.

The leprous man knelt down and begged. So many times today, I've prayed that God would spare me cancer. Like the friends of the paralyzed man—who cut a hole in the roof and lowered him to Jesus's feet (Mark 2:2–4)—my friends have been pleading with the Lord for me as well. But just as Jesus showed before he healed the paralyzed man, forgiveness for my sins is even more important than my body here and now. If Jesus made me, I must trust that he knows best and that if I do have cancer, his resurrection life will one day heal my wounds and beautify my scars. I know this because Jesus's own resurrection body—the body he will have for all eternity—is scarred as well. When Jesus met with doubting Thomas, he didn't say, "Look! My crucifixion wounds have gone!" He said, "Put your finger here, and see my hands; and put out your hand, and place it in my side" (John 20:27). If we trust Jesus, he will always heal us in the end. But death may be a stop along the way.

Bleeding and Dying

The leper's request to Jesus sounds strange to us. Why did he ask to be made *clean* instead of *well*? According to Jewish law, lepers were ceremonially "unclean"—not just literally infectious but unable to participate in temple worship. Other things could make you temporarily unclean. Drinking from the same cup as the Samaritan woman would have made Jesus unclean. Touching a dead body would make you unclean. Emissions of bodily fluids made both men and women unclean, so women were unclean during their period. In fact, even touching a menstruating woman would have made you unclean. This context sheds light on a double healing miracle in Matthew, Mark, and Luke.

First, a man called Jairus falls at Jesus's feet and begs, "My little daughter is at the point of death. Come and lay your hands on her, so that she may be made well and live" (Mark 5:23). Jesus sets off with him at once. The crowd is pressing around. But the Gospel authors zoom in on one woman in the throng: a woman who's been bleeding for twelve years: as long as Jairus's girl has been alive. This woman had "suffered much under many physicians, and had spent all that she had, and was no better but rather grew worse" (Mark 5:26). At this point, she is desperate and destitute. So she sneaks up on Jesus and touches his clothes, "For she said, 'If I touch even his garment, I will be made well'" (5:28). Immediately, the woman felt the bleeding stop. No doubt, she was hoping she could melt back into the crowd. For twelve years, she has been unclean and now she's touched this famous rabbi. Pray God no one finds out! But Jesus, perceiving that power had gone out from him, asks, "Who touched my garments?" (5:30)

The disciples respond, "You see the crowd pressing around you, and yet you say, 'Who touched me?'" (5:31). But Jesus won't let it go. When the woman saw she could not hide, she "came in fear and trembling and fell down before him and told him the whole truth" (5:33). This woman was shaking with fear. What did she think she was doing touching Jesus in her condition? But Jesus has no rebuke for her, just tenderness: "Daughter, your faith has made you well; go in peace, and be healed of your disease" (5:34). Jairus is desperately worried about his literal daughter. But Jesus recognizes the woman who has touched him as a daughter who has faith in him: the kind of faith that knows that however unclean you are, just touching the hem of Jesus's clothes can transform you. Too often, people think they need to clean themselves up before coming to Jesus. Shed the alcohol problem. Kick the pornography addiction. Exit that bad relationship and then come. But Jesus knows all our shame—be it physical or moral—and he wants us as we are. Trying to clean ourselves up before coming to him is like trying to get well before going to the doctor.

The words of tenderness to the bleeding woman have hardly died on Jesus's lips when someone from Jairus's house arrives. "Your daughter is dead," he says. "Why trouble the Teacher any further?" (Mark 5:35). But Jesus says to Jairus, "Do not fear; only believe" (5:36). When they get to his house, people are mourning for the little girl, but Jesus says, "Why are you making a commotion and weeping? The child is not dead but sleeping" (5:39). They laugh at him. Who does Jesus think he's kidding? Touching a dead body would make you unclean as well. But Jesus takes this dead girl by the hand and says in their shared mother tongue: "'Talitha cumi' which means 'Little girl, I say to you, arise'" (5:41). Immediately, the girl gets up. Jesus tells her family to keep it quiet and to give her something to eat (5:42–43). This bleeding woman and this dead girl could no more make Jesus unclean than a speck of dust could blot out the sun. But he could make them well.

Unworthy

Dreamed up by L'Oreal in 1971, the slogan, "Because I'm worth it," has been translated into forty languages. It's still going strong fifty years later, because it codifies a modern mantra: believe in yourself. Low self-esteem is the great dragon we must fight today with weapons put into our hands by companies that claim to know we're worth their merchandise. But it's striking that in the Gospels, the people most drawn to Jesus believe the opposite.

In Matthew 8, right after Jesus heals the leper, a Roman centurion comes to Jesus saying, "Lord, my servant is lying paralyzed at home, suffering terribly" (Matt. 8:6). The centurion was a Gentile and a man of social status. He had a hundred men under his command. Jesus says he'll come and heal his servant (8:7). But the centurion replies, "Lord, I am not worthy to have you come under my roof, but only say the word, and my servant will be healed" (8:8). He knows that Jesus can command his servant's sickness to stop, just as he himself can tell his soldiers what to do (8:9). Jesus doesn't need to come to give the word. In fact, this centurion believes he's not remotely worthy to have Jesus in his home.

Jesus is so impressed with this centurion that he turns to his Jewish disciples and says,

> Truly, I tell you, with no one in Israel have I found such faith. I tell you, many will come from east and west and recline at table with Abraham, Isaac, and Jacob in the kingdom of heaven, while the sons of the kingdom will be thrown into outer darkness. In that place there will be weeping and gnashing of teeth. (8:10–12)

According to the messianic expectations of his day, Jesus was meant to throw centurions out. But here is Jesus welcoming them in—if they will humbly put their trust in him. In fact, Jesus says here that many Gentiles will enter the kingdom of heaven while many of his fellow Jews will be thrown out for failing to acknowledge him. But this was not from any anti-Jewish sentiment. Quite the reverse. Jesus consistently went to Jewish settlements first. But when non-Jewish people came to him, he never turned them away.

Except for once.

Feeding the Dogs

I grew up in a village near Windsor, where the Queen of England lives. Our local village church used centuries-old Anglican prayers.

My favorite one begins like this: "We do not presume to come to this thy table, O merciful Lord, trusting in our own righteousness, but in thy manifold and great mercies. We are not worthy so much as to gather up the crumbs under thy table."[1] I did not know it at the time, but this prayer was inspired by a woman who lived almost two thousand years ago: a Gentile woman begging for help.

First, we see Jesus wrangling with the Pharisees and scribes. They complain that Jesus's disciples aren't ceremonially washing their hands before they eat. He says they're the ones who are really failing to follow God's commands and quotes Isaiah against them:

> This people honors me with their lips,
> but their heart is far from me. (Mark 7:6)

Then Jesus explains that it's not unclean food going into someone's stomach that defiles them but the evil that comes out of his or her heart (7:14–23). This teaching tramples down a Jew-Gentile divide. As if to make his point with his feet as well as with his mouth, Jesus got up and left for the predominantly Gentile region of Tyre and Sidon (7:24).

As soon as he got there, "a woman whose little daughter had an unclean spirit heard of him and came and fell down at his feet" (Mark 7:25). Mark calls her "a Gentile, a Syrophoenician by birth" (7:26). Matthew calls her "a Canaanite woman" (Matt. 15:22). Is this a contradiction? No. The Canaanites were the original inhabitants of the land God promised to the Jews. Matthew is connecting this

1 Known as the "Prayer of Humble Access," it was included in the *Book of Common Prayer* of the Church of England under the editorial hand of Thomas Cranmer in the sixteenth century. This wording reflects the 1662 edition. See *The 1662 Book of Common Prayer: International Edition*, ed. Samuel L. Bray and Drew Nathaniel Keene (Downers Grove, IL: IVP Academic, 2021), 261.

woman with the people the Israelites displaced on God's command. She's a paradigmatic outsider. And yet she pleads, "Have mercy on me, O Lord, Son of David; my daughter is severely oppressed by a demon" (Matt. 15:22). Jesus doesn't answer. His disciples ask him to send her away. Jesus's response leaves the situation hanging: "I was sent only to the lost sheep of the house of Israel" (15:24). But the woman comes and kneels before him begging, "Lord, help me" (15:25). Time and again, Jesus healed when he was asked, but this time his response is shocking: "It is not right to take the children's bread and throw it to the dogs" (15:26).

The Old Testament often calls God's people his "children." Jesus says the Jews should be fed first and uses a derogatory term Jews sometimes used for Gentiles. To be sure, the word for dog that Jesus uses has more positive connotations than the canine word he could have used. But still, it's not a compliment. His Jewish disciples would likely have applauded: Jews first! But just as Jesus's question to the rich young man—"Why do you call me good?"—invited his audience to think more deeply, so his response to this woman is intended to expose a countercultural truth. And it does. "Yes, Lord," the woman replies, "yet even the dogs eat the crumbs that fall from their masters' table" (Matt. 15:27). Jesus responds, "'O woman, great is your faith! Be it done for you as you desire.' And her daughter was healed instantly" (15:28).

Some people think this woman changed Jesus's mind about the Gentiles. But this makes no sense. As we saw earlier, Jesus had already healed the servant of a Roman centurion and commented on how the Gentiles were coming into his kingdom when many of the sons of the kingdom were not. Just like the Roman centurion, the bleeding woman, the dead girl, and the leper, Jesus thought this woman was worth it. But in each of these stories we see that coming to Jesus is like entering the most beautiful underground cave: to get in we must first get down on our hands and knees. Then he will lift us up and show us all the wonders that are found in him.

Perhaps you're thinking, "Didn't we miss the weirdest part of this story? Angels announcing Jesus's birth was bad enough, but are you expecting me to believe in *demons* now?" I get it. Angels and demons are pretty remote from my day-to-day experience too. In modern, Western culture, we tend to believe that humans are essentially good and that extravagantly evil acts must be the result of bad education or untreated mental illness. There's space in a biblical worldview for each of these causes of wrong. But in the Gospels, we see evil springing from two other sources too. First, the human heart itself. Second, spiritual forces that are hostile to God. This diagnosis of the causes of evil leaves us grappling with an unflattering view of humanity and a culturally alien belief in evil spirits. But if we reason away all evil as simply poor education or mental illness, we ultimately rob ourselves of the reality of good. If my envy and my meanness are simply products of my brain composition and life experiences, then my attempts at generosity and kindness are no more than that as well. When we close the door to the reality of hate, the door to real love shuts quietly behind us too.[2]

Healing the Spiritually Sick

In J. R. R. Tolkien's *The Return of the King*, a fight with the evil Witch-king of Angmar has left my favorite character—Éowyn—on the verge of death. Her wounds are physical, but also spiritual. The good wizard Gandalf declares that only in the coming of Aragorn does any hope remain. He quotes an ancient prophecy:

2 For more on this point, see Rebecca McLaughlin, *Confronting Christianity: 12 Hard Questions for the World's Largest Religion* (Wheaton, IL: Crossway, 2019), 209–21.

"*The hands of the king are the hands of a healer.*"[3] Aragorn doesn't look much like a king. He's lived for decades as a wanderer without a home. But at this point in the book, he's made his claim to be the rightful king of Gondor, and part of the proof that he *is* the rightful king is that he's able to heal the physically and spiritually sick.

We might wonder if the Gospels only talk about people being possessed by demons or "unclean spirits" because in those days, people didn't understand mental illness or conditions like epilepsy. But if we read the Gospels carefully, we'll find that the same physical symptoms (for example, inability to hear or speak) are sometimes attributed to unclean spirits and sometimes to sickness. From Jesus's perspective, "This person has a demon," wasn't a catch-all diagnosis.

When Jesus exorcises demons, he's not going on a witch hunt, casting problematic people out. Instead, he's on a search-and-rescue mission, bringing hurting people in. In a particularly striking episode in Luke, Jesus heals a man who has been overwhelmed by many demons and has been living naked and violent among the tombs. "What have you to do with me, Jesus, Son of the Most High God?" the man cries out. "I beg you, do not torment me" (Luke 8:28). The destructive power of the demons is so great that when Jesus orders them to leave the man and to enter a nearby herd of pigs, the pigs immediately drown themselves in a lake. The pig herders run off and tell everyone what's happened. When people come to see the formerly destructive man, they find him sitting peacefully at Jesus's feet, dressed and in his right mind (8:32–35).

Rather than praising God for this extraordinary transformation, the people are "seized with great fear," and they ask Jesus to leave their region (8:37). But the healed man begs that Jesus would take

3 J. R. R. Tolkien, *The Return of the King* (New York: Ballantine, 2012), 142 (italics original).

him with him. Like Mary Magdalene—one of Jesus's most famous followers, who had been healed from seven demons (8:2)—this man is ready to follow Jesus wherever he goes. But Jesus has a different plan for him: "Return to your home, and declare how much God has done for you" (8:39). So, the man goes away, "proclaiming throughout the whole city how much Jesus had done for him" (8:40). Notice Luke's sleight of hand, replacing "God" with "Jesus" here? Luke *is* telling us. And oddly, so are the demons.

In *The Lord of the Rings*, whenever the hobbit Frodo puts on the ring, he's able to see the evil spiritual beings he's fighting against. The ring gives him a kind of spiritual sight: like night vision. Likewise, when evil spirits are confronted with Jesus in the Gospels, they seem to know exactly who he is—and they're terrified. The first demon-possessed man we meet in Mark cries out with a voice that's not his own, "What have you to do with us, Jesus of Nazareth? Have you come to destroy us? I know who you are—the Holy One of God" (Mark 1:24). Jesus responds, "Be silent, and come out of him!" (1:25). Mark summarizes later: "whenever the unclean spirits saw him, they fell down before him and cried out, 'You are the Son of God.' And he strictly ordered them not to make him known" (3:11–12).[4]

As we saw in chapter 3, Jesus guarded his identity as the Messiah carefully, until the time was right. When spirits shout out who he is, he shuts them up. But they're right about Jesus, and they're right to be afraid. When Aragorn first confronts the Witch-king of Angmar and his fellow ring wraiths, he wields a flaming torch to force them back. But Jesus doesn't need a torch. Jesus himself is the light of the world: beating back the darkness, poised to destroy

4 See also Mark 1:34 and Luke 4:41.

evil in the most surprising way. But human beings tangled up in evil aren't collateral damage. They're mission-critical assets worth the operative's life.

Who Sinned?

When my firstborn was two, I caught her spitting on her hands and rubbing her saliva on her highchair tray. "Miranda, that's disgusting!" I responded. "We don't spit!" She eyed me a condescending gaze and said, "Jesus once used a lot of spit to do a very great miracle." She was right. But before rubbing saliva mixed with mud on a blind man's eyes to heal him, Jesus had a striking conversation.

When his disciples saw a blind man begging, they ask Jesus, "Rabbi, who sinned, this man or his parents, that he was born blind?" (John 9:2). In Jesus's day, many Jews believed that physical conditions were a consequence of sin. In one sense, they weren't wrong. The Bible teaches that we humans are gloriously made in the image of God but that we're riddled with sin from head to toe. According to the biblical narrative, all that's wrong in this world—from Kalashnikovs to cancer—is a consequence of our rejecting God. So you can understand the disciples' question. But Jesus says they've got it all wrong: "It was not that this man sinned, or his parents, but that the works of God might be displayed in him" (9:3)

Of course, there may be times in our own lives when sinful actions have caused sickness. A Christian friend of mine struggles with alcoholism. He mostly manages to stay dry, but every now and then, the struggle gets too much, and he goes on a binge that lands him in the hospital. Our choices *can* have physical consequences. But often, when we suffer physically, it's not a consequence of our sin. I'm texting with a friend right now who's had a barrage of debilitating sicknesses crop up in quick succession—to the point that she feels like she's playing whack-a-mole with her body. Like you and me, she is a sinner. But her sickness isn't caused by her sin. If it turns out that I have cancer, it will no more be evidence of my sin than it will be evidence of my goodness if I don't. In fact, when Jesus heals this blind man, we find that he's more spiritually healthy than the Pharisees.

"As long as I am in the world, I am the light of the world," Jesus declares. Then he spits on the ground and makes some mud with his saliva (John 9:5–6). He rubs the mud onto the blind man's eyes and tells him to go and wash in the pool of Siloam. When he comes back, he can see. Jesus usually healed just with a word or a touch. But here he takes a physically involved path to healing this man, even while saying he is the light of the world. The people who have seen the blind man begging all his life wonder what happened. They take him to the Pharisees, who don't believe he's been healed. They call his parents in to see if this is *really* their blind son. His parents say he is. But they're too scared to answer questions about Jesus, so they point the Pharisees back to their son (9:7–23).

Courageously, the formerly blind man points out to them that Jesus must have come from God, or else he could not have healed him. They're furious. "You were born in utter sin," they say, "and would you teach us?" (9:34). Then they throw him out. But Jesus goes to find the man and asks, "Do you believe in the Son of Man?" (9:35). The man asks, "And who is he, sir, that I may believe in him?" Jesus replies, "You have seen him, and it is he who is speaking to you (9:36–37). "Lord, I believe," replies the man, and he worships Jesus. Then Jesus says, "For judgment I came into this world, that those who do not see may see, and those who see may become blind" (9:38–39). Some of the Pharisees hear him and ask, "Are we also blind?" Jesus replies, "If you were blind, you would have no guilt; but now that you say, 'We see,' your guilt remains" (9:40–41).

Time and again in the Gospels, people who know they're physically sick come to Jesus for healing and life. Time and again, people who think they are spiritually well reject him. The blind man *was* born in utter sin. But so were the Pharisees. His spiritual sight is better than theirs, so he can see Jesus for who he really is.

He Took Our Illnesses

I'd somehow imagined that my husband would be able to be with me while they took the biopsies. I'd told myself he'd hold my hand, and it would be ok. I almost never cry in front of people. But when we got to the doctor's surgery, they said Bryan couldn't come in. I cried. I cried as I walked in. I cried as I was asked a litany of health-history questions. I cried as I lay down and the doctor prepared her tools. And then I started singing in my head a song we sometimes sing at church:

> Whom shall I fear? Whom shall I fear?
> The Lord is the strength of my life.[5]

If I do have cancer, Bryan will hold my hand as best he can. But he won't be able to come into the operating theater. He'll be shut out of many spaces where I suffer pain and fear, and in the end, he won't be able to take my sickness away. But according to the Gospels, Jesus is with us always, to the very end of time (Matt. 28:20), and he's taken all our sickness on himself.

5 Lillian Bouknight, "The Lord Is My Light" (Jackson, MS: Savgos Music, 1980).

After telling us that Jesus healed many people in one evening—both those who were oppressed by spirits and those who were physically sick—Matthew observes, "This was to fulfill what was spoken by the prophet Isaiah: 'He took our illnesses and bore our diseases'" (8:17). The verses from Isaiah read,

> Surely he has borne our griefs
> and carried our sorrows;
> yet we esteemed him stricken,
> smitten by God, and afflicted.
> But he was pierced for our transgressions;
> he was crushed for our iniquities;
> upon him was the chastisement that brought us peace,
> and with his wounds we are healed. (Isa. 53:4–5)

Jesus's death on the cross is bound up with his power to heal. He came to take our sickness, physical and spiritual, upon himself. He came to hold us as we suffer from cancer, AIDS, depression, COVID–19, or chronic, untreatable pain. He came to gather all our sicknesses, peeling them away from us and sticking them upon himself. He came to have his body broken so that we might be completely whole one day when he returns to earth again.

So What?

I'd just loaded my kids, all wet from swimming, into the car when the doctor called. "Good news," she said, "We don't think you have cancer." This time, Jesus's answer to "If you will, you can make me clean" was "I will." But my younger friend who also trusts in Jesus is going through another hateful round of chemotherapy this week. One day, the answer for me will be different as well. Most likely, one day, I'll be headed to the hospital again. The doors will close on me. The curtains will be drawn. The instruments will multiply, and I won't leave. When that day comes, I'll need the resurrection life that no doctor other than Jesus can give.

If there are evil forces in this world, we need an overwhelming, demon-crushing, darkness-killing champion. We need someone who'll separate us out from darkness and wrap us up in light. We need the doctor who can heal our bodies and our souls, the doctor who can take our pain, the doctor who can even raise the dead. Jesus in the Gospels heals with words and touch and spit. The hands of the King are the hands of a healer. But this King was mocked and hit and spat upon as he went to the cross where he took our illnesses and bore our diseases. He died almost two thousand years ago, but his scarred, healing hands reach out for you and me today—if we will only come to him.

5

Jesus the Teacher

I WAS SITTING in a coffee shop in small-town Missouri. My conversation partner was a woman sporting multicolored hair and gay pride accessories. She identified as LGBTQ: specifically, pansexual. She'd had a serious girlfriend for several years and was now in a polyamorous relationship with two men. That morning, I'd spoken on gender and sexuality at a nearby church. Some local activists had organized a protest. But this woman had come to hear me out. She'd asked a thoughtful question and had kindly agreed to meet for coffee to talk more. As we chatted, I found that she'd listened very carefully. It wasn't quite the message she'd expected. I've always experienced same-sex attraction myself, so she knew I wasn't speaking out of ignorance or prejudice. At one point, she said, "So what I think you were saying is that people don't go to hell because they're gay. They go to hell because they haven't hidden themselves in Jesus." I said, "That's right."

Jesus in the Gospels doesn't fit our modern paradigms. His attacks on the rich and his protection of the poor make most left-wing leaders look like heartless fat cats. But his teachings about sexual sin make most conservatives look soft. Jesus talks more about love across differences and inclusion for the marginalized than the most tenderhearted liberal. And yet he issues terrifying warnings of God's judgment. He eviscerates those who think they're swaying God with their religiousness. And yet he says that loving God trumps everything. He calls us not to judge lest we be judged. And yet he says that one day he will judge us all. Jesus's moral standards are so high that we haven't a hope in hell of reaching them. And yet he welcomes the most abject moral failures.

Each chapter in this book depends on Jesus's teaching, and this chapter gives an utterly inadequate account of what he said. If that frustrates you, good—put this book down and pick a Gospel up. This volume is, at best, a warm-up act. But my hope in the next few pages is to tune your senses into this first-century Jewish rabbi's words by giving you a flavor of his teaching style and a taste of what he said on three key themes that still preoccupy us today: love across differences, money, and sex. We'll see that Jesus's teachings are not freestanding moral truths. They are inseparable from who he is. And they're the basis for the moral truths we hold to be self-evident today.

Did Jesus Really Mean That?

I often tell my kids, "I'll have your guts for garters if you . . ." It's my favorite British threat. Of course, I wouldn't really do it. But they get the general drift. If they do what I've warned them not to do and say, "I knew you didn't mean that *literally*," I wouldn't be impressed.

If you read the Gospels, you'll find that Jesus often used nonliteral language to deliver truth. He sprayed his audience with metaphors and parables and often detonated hyperbole: extreme exaggeration for rhetorical effect. When Jesus said to the religious hypocrites, "You blind guides, straining out a gnat and swallowing a camel!" (Matt. 23:24), he did not mean that they were *literally* ingesting camels but that their understanding of God's law was so point-missing that they might as well be. Likewise, Jesus's oft-quoted warning, "Judge not, that you be not judged" (Matt. 7:1), is followed by a similarly graphic question:

> Why do you see the speck that is in your brother's eye, but do not notice the log that is in your own eye? Or how can you say to your brother, "Let me take the speck out of your eye," when there is the log in your own eye? You hypocrite, first take the log out of your own eye, and then you will see clearly to take the speck out of your brother's eye. (Matt. 7:3–5)

Even with our modern, Western eyes, we see what Jesus means. Our willingness to judge when we ourselves are wrapped around with sin is as absurd as someone with a tree stuck in his cornea thinking he could help get a speck of sawdust out of someone else's eye. In a culture like ours that prides itself on being non-judgmental, this kind of teaching goes down well. But often Jesus's use of hyperbole is more unsettling.

Seeing that great crowds were following him, Jesus said, "If anyone comes to me and does not hate his own father and mother and wife and children and brothers and sisters, yes, and even his own life, he cannot be my disciple" (Luke 14:26). If this were all we knew of Jesus's teaching, we might think he was calling us to hate our families. But Jesus criticizes his religious antagonists for neglecting their parents (Mark 7:10–13); he defends marriage so strongly that even his disciples are shocked (Matt. 19:1–12); he values children in a way that changed their status ever afterwards (Matt. 19:13–15). So what does Jesus mean when he says you cannot follow him if you don't hate your family? He means that love of any other person *in comparison to Jesus* should be tantamount to hate.

Words like these fit very poorly with the secular liberal "Jesus was just a good teacher" hypothesis. He's calling us to worship him, forsaking every other claim. If Jesus is not God, this demand is not good. But Jesus in the Gospels also can't be squeezed into the typically conservative mold. He's not a nice, religious add-on to family values. If you just want marriage and two-point-four kids with church on Sunday for that warm and fuzzy feeling, you can't have Jesus. He wants *you*, heart and soul, not your spare time, spare cash, and spare religious sentiment. But if we give up everything for Jesus, we'll end up loving those around us more. In fact, instead of hating those we're primed to love, we'll end up loving those we're primed to hate.

The Good . . . Samaritan?

One day, a Jewish lawyer questioned Jesus: "Teacher, what shall I do to inherit eternal life?" (Luke 10:25). Jesus replied, "What is written in the Law? How do you read it?" The lawyer answered, "You shall love the Lord your God with all your heart and with all your soul and with all your strength and with all your mind, and your neighbor as yourself" (10:26–27). Jesus replied, "You have answered correctly; do this and you will live" (10:28). But the lawyer had a follow-up: "And who is my neighbor?" (10:29). That's when Jesus landed the scandalous story of the good Samaritan.

In Jesus's story, a man is walking from Jerusalem to Jericho when he gets robbed and left for dead. First, a Jewish priest walks by. Seeing the beaten man, he crosses the road—not to help, but to avoid him. Two years ago, a friend of mine was robbed and assaulted and left to bleed out by the side of a walkway near my house. But when a stranger came along, he called an ambulance and saved her life. The priest in Jesus's story leaves the injured man to die. Next, a Levite (a priest's assistant) passes by and does the same. Finally, a Samaritan picks up the dying man and cares for him at great personal cost.

If we read this parable with our modern, Western eyes, we'll find a powerful story about loving helpless strangers. We'll notice (perhaps with satisfaction) that it's told against religious leaders. But what's lost in translation today is the aspect of the story that would have screamed to Jesus's first audience: the hero of the story is a Samaritan. It's like telling a story to White folk during segregation in the South in which a Black man was the moral hero. Or like telling a story to the Democratic National Convention in which a Republican senator saved the day. Jesus's story made such waves that even folks who've never heard of it talk about someone being a "good Samaritan," and an international suicide prevention organization is named "Samaritans." Jesus's story rips apart the lawyer's categories for humans he must love. His care must not be circumscribed by ethnic or religious boundaries. Of course, Jesus could have made this point with a story of a Jew loving a Samaritan. But instead he reversed the moral flow, casting someone his fellow Jews saw as ethnically *inferior* as being ethically *superior*.

We all feel good when folks on our side are noble enough to love their enemies. For example, I recently read a news article on an LGBT advocacy site about gay people on a boat being harassed by homophobic bigots—until the bigots' boat caught fire, at which point the gay folks rescued them. The site would likely not have told the story if the roles had been reversed. But Jesus does. Loving your neighbor means loving people you were raised to *hate*. It means loving across racial, ethnic, cultural, and religious differences. It means spending your money and risking your life to stop on a dangerous road and help the needy person *least* like you—a person your friends would avoid like the plague, a person raised to hate your guts.

Jesus underlines this teaching in his famous Sermon on the Mount: "You have heard that it was said, 'You shall love your neighbor and hate your enemy.' But I say to you, Love your enemies and pray for those who persecute you" (Matt. 5:43–44). These words sound nice to you and me. Perhaps we'll be a little kinder to that irritating guy at work. But I'm writing this on the day that Kabul was taken by the Taliban. These words of Jesus mean that Christians in Afghanistan today are called to love the Taliban. According to Jesus, this kind of shocking, costly, universal love is not a moral nice-to-have. It's central to God's ethical concern. And so it can't be peeled away from loving God with all your heart and mind and soul and strength. If the priest and the Levite had truly loved God, they would have loved the beaten man as well.

I shared this story with my new, pansexual friend. She'd never heard of it. But I explained that the beliefs we both held dear—our belief in human equality regardless of race or sex or health, our belief that the poor should be provided for and the oppressed protected, our belief in love across racial and cultural differences—all come from the teachings of a first-century Jewish rabbi known as Jesus of Nazareth. The story of the good Samaritan is one plank in the ethical raft that Jesus built, the raft that supports all our beliefs about human equality, a raft we've all been floating on—and falling off—ever since. If we reject this ancient raft, we don't find a secular lifeboat with a modern scientific motor engine to support these deep beliefs. We drown.

Equality Comes from Christianity

You may think the claim that human equality comes from Jesus is just my super-biased, Christian take—like the father in *My Big Fat Greek Wedding* who claims that everything comes from Greece. ("Give me a word, any word, and I show you that the root of that word is Greek.")[1] But when British historian Tom Holland set out to write *Dominion: How the Christian Revolution Remade the World*, he was not a Christian.[2] He'd always been far more attracted by the Greek and Roman gods than by the crucified hero of Christianity. But through years of research, he concluded that he—agnostic as he was—held many specifically Christian beliefs: for example, his belief in universal human equality and the need to care for the poor and oppressed.

What about questions of gender and sexuality: the issues on which my pansexual friend and I directly disagreed? Even here, Holland argues, folks on all sides pitch their tent on Christian soil:

> That every human being possessed an equal dignity was not remotely a self-evident truth. A Roman would have laughed at it. To campaign against discrimination on the grounds of gender or sexuality, however, was to depend on large numbers of people sharing in a common assumption: that everyone possessed an inherent worth. The origins of this principle—as Nietzsche had

1 *My Big Fat Greek Wedding*, directed by Joel Zwick (Beverly Hills, CA: Gold Circle Films, 2002).

2 Tom Holland, *Dominion: How the Christian Revolution Remade the World* (New York: Basic, 2019).

contemptuously pointed out—lay not in the French Revolution, nor in the Declaration of Independence, nor in the Enlightenment, but in the Bible.[3]

Of course, if the kind of love across differences that Jesus taught through the parable of the good Samaritan was all the Bible had to say on ethics, my conversation in Missouri would have been easier. I'd only have been telling her that Jesus was the source for things she already believed. But what about the ways in which Christianity collides with many people's deeply held beliefs about both sex and sexuality? Is it true, as some folks claim, that Jesus doesn't care about whom we sleep with?

People sometimes glean this from Jesus's well-known love for sexual sinners. He befriended a Samaritan woman who had had five husbands and was now cohabiting (John 4:1–30). He protected a woman caught in adultery (John 8:1–11). He welcomed "a woman of the city, who was a sinner" (Luke 7:37). But if we read the Gospels as a whole, we find that Jesus's constant, tender, scandalous welcoming of sexual sinners isn't because he doesn't care about sexual sin.

You Have Heard That It Was Said

Last Sunday we had friends around for lunch. My husband put a chicken in to roast and set a timer while we went to church. When we got home, the house smelled sumptuous. We looked inside the oven, and the chicken looked all crispy and delicious. But when we sliced it up, we found that only the outside inch was cooked. The inside was all pink and raw: inedible and even dangerous to

3 Holland, *Dominion*, 494.

eat. Today, especially when it comes to sexuality, we see discovering our authentic self as the goal. If I just look inside myself and shed all my pretense and all societal constraint, I'll find what's good and beautiful. In my case, my ongoing capacity for attraction to other women must be good. It comes so naturally. You could say that it's my inner truth. But Jesus turns this thinking on its head. Declaring that it's what comes out of our hearts, not what we eat, that makes us unclean before God, he explains, "For from within, out of the heart of man, come evil thoughts, sexual immorality, theft, murder, adultery, coveting, wickedness, deceit, sensuality, envy, slander, pride, foolishness" (Mark 7:21–22). When Jesus takes a slice out of our hearts, exposing our most authentic self, what he sees is about as raw as my husband's uncooked chicken—and the consequences are far more serious.

Among a host of other kinds of sin, Jesus uses two words to allude to sexual sin: *porneia* (the word translated "sexual immorality") and adultery. So long as it's consensual, many today see sex outside marriage as only being wrong if it's adultery: deceitful unfaithfulness versus healthy exploration of our sexuality. But Jesus makes clear that cheating on your husband or your wife is not the only form of sexual sin. Jesus also radically expands what we might think of as adultery. In the middle of his Sermon on the Mount, perhaps the most transformative passage of moral teaching in history, Jesus hits us with this: "You have heard that it was said, 'You shall not commit adultery.' But I say to you that everyone who looks at a woman with lustful intent has already committed adultery with her in his heart" (Matt. 5:27–28).

"You shall not commit adultery" was one of the Ten Commandments. Far from loosening this call to sexual faithfulness, Jesus tightens it. He pinpoints the heart not because our deeds don't matter, but because they're symptoms of a deeper problem. I don't know about you, but I've looked at women with desire in my heart—both before and after marriage—so I've committed adultery in Jesus's eyes. No doubt his words apply to lusting after men as well.

We can imagine Jesus's audience shifting awkwardly in their sandals as he spoke. But like discovering your car's been towed when you thought you'd only get a ticket, it gets worse:

> If your right eye causes you to sin, tear it out and throw it away. For it is better that you lose one of your members than that your whole body be thrown into hell. And if your right hand causes you to sin, cut it off and throw it away. For it is better that you lose one of your members than that your whole body go into hell. (Matt. 5:29–30)

Here Jesus lands two terrifying points. First, the extreme seriousness of sin—sexual and otherwise. Sin earns us all a ticket straight to hell. We're better being maimed than getting on that train. But second, if we read this in the context of Jesus's teachings as a whole, we find that it's not our eyes or our hands that cause us to sin. It's our heart. The rot has gone so deep that there's no part of us that's salvageable. So, what on earth are we to do? This diagnosis leaves us desperate for Jesus the healer. He really is our only hope. And if we come to him, he'll welcome us with open arms.

One day, Jesus was having dinner at a Pharisee's house when "a woman of the city, who was a sinner," came in and fell at his feet (Luke 7:37). She poured ointment on them, kissed them, washed them with her tears, and wiped them with her hair. The Pharisee was appalled: "If this man were a prophet, he would have known who and what sort of woman this is who is touching him, for she is a sinner" (7:39). But Jesus did know. And far from shaming the woman for her actions, he told a parable to shame the Pharisee. "A certain moneylender had two debtors. One owed five hundred denarii, and the other fifty. When they could not pay, he cancelled the debt of both. Now which of them will love him more?" (7:41–42). After the Pharisee gave the right answer, Jesus pointed out the ways in which the Pharisee had failed to show him hospitality and how the woman had made up for his failures with her love. Jesus concluded, "Therefore I tell you, her sins, which are many, are forgiven—for she loved much. But he who is forgiven little, loves little." And he said to the woman, "Your sins are forgiven" (7:47–48). His fellow dinner guests started asking each other, "Who is this, who even forgives sins?" (7:49) But rather than engaging with them, Jesus kept his focus on the woman: "Your faith has saved you," he assured her. "Go in peace" (7:50).

In chapter 6, we'll see what Jesus says about male-female marriage and how it connects to his claim that he himself is the ultimate bridegroom. But here we simply need to recognize that Jesus's teaching on sexual sin is thoroughly offensive. It goes against our every modern instinct about affirmation—of ourselves and others. Like the sinful woman of the city, if we want to come to Jesus, we must wash his feet with our tears. But his teaching on money is even more offensive.

The Rich Man and Lazarus

My family in England kept raving about the TV show *The Good Place*, but I wasn't interested. A comedy about people in the afterlife? It seemed too deathly serious a subject for jokes. When I finally succumbed and started watching it, however, I got their enthusiasm. It's very funny. But it also explores deep truths regarding the ways in which many people think about heaven and hell. In the opening scene, the main character, Eleanor, is told she's died, but that everything is fine. She's in the Good Place. As the action continues, however, Eleanor realizes she's been misassigned. The other people in the Good Place are *exceptionally* good. She knows she's actually quite bad, and it's only a matter of time before she's found out.[4]

If you read through the Gospels, you may start to feel like Eleanor—not only when it comes to sex but also when Jesus starts talking about money. Perhaps you felt a twinge of discomfort when Jesus told the rich young man to give everything he had to the poor and follow him. But he's not done. "Blessed are you who are poor," Jesus said, "for yours is the kingdom of God" (Luke 6:20). "But woe to you who are rich, for you have received your consolation" (6:24). "It is easier for a camel to go through the eye of a needle," Jesus famously proclaimed, "than for a rich person to enter the kingdom of God" (Matt. 19:24; Mark 10:25; Luke 18:25). I could go on and on. But the words I personally find hardest to read come in the form of a parable.

Jesus begins,

> There was a rich man who was clothed in purple and fine linen and who feasted sumptuously every day. And at his gate was laid a poor man named Lazarus, covered with sores, who desired to be fed with what fell from the rich man's table. Moreover, even the dogs came and licked his sores. (Luke 16:19–21)

4 *The Good Place*, season 1, episode 1, "Everything Is Fine," written by Michael Schur, aired September 19, 2016, on NBC.

The contrast of rich and poor is painfully clear. According to Old Testament law, the rich man should have taken care of Lazarus. He doesn't. But Lazarus's name means, "God helps," and Jesus tells us how. "The poor man died," he said, "and was carried by the angels to Abraham's side" (16:22). Lazarus has landed a top spot in the afterlife. So far, so good. We probably all like the idea of poor and suffering people going to a better place. But then comes the blow: "The rich man also died and was buried, and in Hades, being in torment, he lifted up his eyes and saw Abraham far off and Lazarus at his side. . . . 'Father Abraham, have mercy on me, and send Lazarus to dip the end of his finger in water and cool my tongue, for I am in anguish in this flame'" (16:22–24). Here Jesus the fire-and-brimstone preacher gives us a terrifying vision of hell. Abraham replies,

> Child, remember that you in your lifetime received your good things, and Lazarus in like manner bad things; but now he is comforted here, and you are in anguish. And besides all this, between us and you a great chasm has been fixed, in order that those who would pass from here to you may not be able, and none may cross from there to us. (Luke 16:25–26)

Having lost hope for himself, the rich man asks, "Then I beg you, father, to send him to my father's house—for I have five brothers—so that he may warn them, lest they also come into this place of torment" (16:27–28). But Abraham replies, "They have Moses and the Prophets; let them hear them" (16:29). The Hebrew Scriptures are chock full of calls to care for the poor and warnings of God's judgment against those who fail to do so. The rich man and his brothers had all the information that they needed. But the rich man argues back, "No, father Abraham, but if someone goes to them from the dead, they will repent." And Abraham responds with words designed to rattle in our ears: "If they do not hear Moses and the Prophets, neither will they be convinced if someone should rise from the dead" (16:30–31).

We may not live in mansions or have beggars dying on our doorsteps. But the richest person of Jesus's day would be amazed at our comforts: our clothes, our food, the kind of healthcare we can access, how we get from place to place. The chances are that if you're reading this book, you're relatively rich. I don't mean you're the richest of your friends. But I'm guessing you have a roof over your head, food on your table, most likely a college degree, perhaps a car. You may not have as much money as you want. But by global standards even today, you're likely rich. Nearly half the world lives on less than $5.50 a day. According to Jesus, if we treat poverty like someone else's problem, we'll find ourselves in the rich man's horrifying shoes. The rich man failed to listen to the Hebrew Scriptures' calls for care of the poor. But we'll have failed to listen to a man who was raised from the dead.

The Sheep and the Goats

In another famous story, Jesus paints a picture of the day when he'll come back to earth as universal King. He said he will divide the nations into two groups, on his right and on his left, "as a shepherd separates the sheep from the goats" (Matt. 25:32). To the sheep on his right, he will say,

> Come, you who are blessed by my Father, inherit the kingdom prepared for you from the foundation of the world. For I was hungry and you gave me food, I was thirsty and you gave me drink, I was a stranger and you welcomed me, I was naked and

> you clothed me, I was sick and you visited me, I was in prison and you came to me. (Matt. 25:34–36)

When the sheep ask when they did these things, Jesus replies, "Truly, I say to you, as you did it to one of the least of these my brothers, you did it to me" (25:37–40). Here we see Jesus's care for Christians who are destitute, sick, or imprisoned. How we treat them is how we treat him.

At this point, we may feel a bit like Eleanor again. She doesn't think that she deserves the Good Place. But the Bad Place? No. "I was a medium person," she says. "I should get to spend eternity in a medium place. Like Cincinnati." But Jesus doesn't have a medium place. He turns to the people on his left and says,

> Depart from me, you cursed, into the eternal fire prepared for the devil and his angels. For I was hungry and you gave me no food, I was thirsty and you gave me no drink, I was a stranger and you did not welcome me, naked and you did not clothe me, sick and in prison and you did not visit me. (Matt. 25:41–43)

Jesus's teaching doubled down on the concern for the poor and dispossessed that was already strongly present in the Old Testament. The waves he made are still lapping on our moral shores today. But this concern stood starkly in contrast to the prevailing moral beliefs of the empire into which Jesus was born. Historian Tom Holland explains this with some Roman history.

The Gods Cared Nothing for the Poor

In 337—quite unexpectedly—the Roman Emperor Constantine converted to Christianity. Despite persecution, Christianity had been spreading throughout the empire for the past three centuries. With Constantine's conversion, it struck at the imperial heart. But his nephew, Julian, rejected Christianity, and when he became emperor in 361, he "committed himself to claiming back from it those who had 'abandoned the ever-living gods for the corpse of the Jew.'" Julian wrote to the high priest of Galatia complaining about the bad PR his favorite goddess Cybele was getting from their charitable failure: "How apparent to everyone it is, and how shameful, that our own people lack support from us, when no Jew ever has to beg, and the impious Galileans [i.e., Christians] support not only their own poor, but ours as well."[5]

Julian tries to ground his complaint in old-time religion. But, as Holland points out, the Greek and Roman gods "cared nothing for the poor": "The heroes of the Iliad, favourites of the gods, golden and predatory, had scorned the weak and downtrodden. So too . . . had philosophers. The starving deserved no sympathy. Beggars were best rounded up and deported."[6]

Jesus's radical teachings about poverty transformed the status of the destitute. His followers cared not only for their own poor but for pagan beggars too. Holland concludes, "The young emperor, sincere though he was in his hatred of 'Galilean' teachings, and in regretting their impact upon all that he held most dear, was blind to the irony of his plan for combatting them: that it was itself irredeemably Christian."[7] He goes on to point out that many today make Julian's mistake. They see Christianity as the enemy of their deepest beliefs about human equality and care for the poor without realizing that those very beliefs are, as Holland puts it, "irredeemably Christian."

5 Quoted in Holland, *Dominion*, 139.

6 Holland, *Dominion*,139.

7 Holland, *Dominion*,139

Come Home!

If prostitutes were the archetypal sexual sinners of Jesus's day, tax collectors were the archetypal financial sinners. Jesus had a magnetic effect on both. Luke tells us that while "the tax collectors and sinners were all drawing near to him," the Pharisees and scribes were complaining: "This man receives sinners and eats with them" (Luke 15:1–2). Jesus responded,

> What man of you, having a hundred sheep, if he has lost one of them, does not leave the ninety-nine in the open country, and go after the one that is lost, until he finds it? And when he has found it, he lays it on his shoulders, rejoicing. And when he comes home, he calls together his friends and his neighbors, saying to them, "Rejoice with me, for I have found my sheep that was lost." Just so, I tell you, there will be more joy in heaven over one sinner who repents than over ninety-nine righteous persons who need no repentance. (15:4–7)

To underline his point, Jesus follows this story with the parable known as the prodigal son. He tells of a young man who asked his father for his inheritance, left his father's house, and squandered the money on reckless living. Finally, he ran out of cash. He found himself tending pigs and longing to eat their swill. This brought him to his senses, and he went back home. Perhaps, if he was lucky, his dad would take him back as a servant. "But while he was still a long way off, his father saw him and felt compassion, and ran and embraced him and kissed him" (15:20). What's more, the father threw a party for his son and welcomed him back without a word of condemnation. This is the vision Jesus gives us for God's eagerness to have us back, however far we've run away from him, however much money we've squandered, however much pornography we've watched, or people we've slept with, or lies we've told, or even folks we've failed to help. He wants us back.

So What?

I don't know how you feel on hearing Jesus's words. Perhaps you feel the justice of Jesus's teaching on care for the poor, but all this talk of sexual sin seems flat repressed, or even harmful. Or maybe you appreciate his words on sexual sin but think his take on caring for the poor is too extreme. Maybe you're a fan of family values, but welcoming destitute foreigners or visiting those in prison sounds like bad policy to you. Like a cross-shaped peg that won't fit in a round hole, the Jesus of the Gospels fails to fit into our categories. But his message is clear: sin of every kind will pave our way to hell. But he will throw his arms around us if we come to him for help.

My new friend in Missouri had drawn a helpful sketch of what she thought she'd heard me say. When Jesus taught, he taught with pictures too: metaphors, stories, hyperbole, and actions. And his message was exactly what she thought she'd heard: we're all going to hell unless we hide ourselves in Jesus. But if we do, we're totally forgiven and caught up into his embrace. Jesus is our lifeline, our escape hatch, our way out. But he's also, as we'll see in chapter 6, our destination.

6

Jesus the Lover

YAA GYASI'S *Homegoing* broke me. It starts in eighteenth-century Ghana and follows the fortunes of two half sisters. One stayed in Ghana and married a white, British slave trader. The other was captured and transported to the New World as a slave. The book switches back and forth between their descendants: one on each side for eight generations. We see the dehumanizing horror of slavery and the aftershock of segregation. We see Ghanaian tribal culture and the impact of white slave traders on local politics. We see hopes and fears, loves and losses piled up and pressed down as Gyasi's pen traces the bloodlines. But the story that broke me was the story of Ness.

Ness was born into slavery in the American South. Her master ("the Devil") assigned her a husband. Recently stolen from Africa, he spoke no English but was nonetheless stamped with an English name: Sam. Forced into marriage, Sam and Ness develop a touching and self-sacrificing love. They have a baby and make plans to escape with the help of a woman they met at the black church they're allowed to visit once a year. But days into their journey north,

Ness senses that the Devil is about to find them, so she passes her baby to their guide. Ness and Sam both give themselves up to save their son. They're captured and returned to the plantation. Ness is mercilessly beaten. Then they lift her head and make her watch her husband being hanged.[1]

This story tears the script of any modern-day romance. While we prize romantic choice above all else, Ness is assigned to a man she's never met—whose words, at first, she cannot understand. And yet their love becomes so real that Sam will sacrifice his life so that their son can escape. In this chapter, we'll meet Jesus the lover. Like Sam, his love is not expressed with flowers, chocolates, and romantic lines. It's written in his blood. And just as Sam loved his wife and his son in different ways, we'll see that Jesus is the true source of different kinds of love: husband to wife, parent to child, friend to friend.

Jesus the Bridegroom

Right now, I'm reading Jane Austen with my elder daughter Miranda. I made the mistake of telling her that all Austen's novels end with marriage. It's a terrible spoiler. She works out by process of elimination who will marry whom. The perfect plots are robbed of their reversals. While writing romances for her heroines, however, Austen chose singleness herself. When she was twenty-six, a twenty-one-year-old friend of the family proposed. At first, it seems that Austen accepted him. But after sleeping on it, she changed her mind. When she died, aged forty-one, it was in her beloved sister's arms.

If you pick up Mark's Gospel and read it without spoilers, there's a moment in chapter 2 when you might wonder if it's also a ro-

1 Yaa Gyasi, *Homegoing* (New York: Vingate, 2016), 87.

mance. After being criticized for spending time with sinners, Jesus is asked why his disciples do not fast. He answers, "Can the wedding guests fast while the bridegroom is with them? As long as they have the bridegroom with them, they cannot fast. The days will come when the bridegroom is taken away from them, and then they will fast in that day" (Mark 2:19–20).

These words don't prophesy a happy ending. It sounds more *Romeo and Juliet* than *Pride and Prejudice*. But nonetheless, Jesus bills himself as the bridegroom. So who is his bride? Read to the end of Mark and you won't find her. Like Austen, Jesus died young and never married. But if you read the prequels to the Gospels, you'll get what he means.

The Old Testament prophets—including Isaiah, Jeremiah, Ezekiel, and Hosea—cast God as a loving, faithful husband and Israel as an often-cheating wife. Hosea was called to marry an unfaithful woman as a picture of God's unrelenting love for Israel (Hos. 1:2–3; 3:1–5). Isaiah declares, "Your Maker is your husband, the Lord of hosts is his name" (Isa. 54:5). Through Jeremiah, God tells his people, "I remember the devotion of your youth, your love as a bride, how you followed me in the wilderness" (Jer. 2:2). But he goes on to accuse them: "You have played the whore with many lovers; and would you return to me?" (Jer. 3:1). Time and again, God's people are found guilty of worshiping other gods and of injustice: "On your skirts is found the lifeblood of the guiltless poor," mourns Jeremiah (2:34). "Surely, as a treacherous wife leaves her husband, so have you been treacherous to me, O house of Israel, declares the Lord" (Jer. 3:20). Ezekiel gives the same diagnosis. Unlike the other nations, God's people did not sacrifice their children. But in his complaint against Jerusalem's idol worship, the Lord accuses her, "You took your sons and your daughters, whom you had borne to me, and these you sacrificed to them to be devoured" (Ezek. 16:20). The spiritual adultery of God's people was chronic and crippling. Repeatedly, God called her back. But the marriage never really seemed to work.

This backstory illuminates the first of Jesus's miracles in John. Jesus and his disciples were guests at a wedding. The wine was running out, and Jesus's mother Mary called on him to intervene. Jesus turned gallons of water into sumptuous wine. The master of the feast assumed that the bridegroom, who was normally responsible for the drinks, had held the best wine back till last (John 2:10). And he was right. But he'd got the bridegroom's identity wrong. Given how many miracles Jesus performed, we might think it odd that John chose this one to record for us. After all, no one was healed. But Jesus stepping into the bridegroom's traditional role at a wedding feast gives us a glimpse of who he truly is.

John the Baptist turned this glimpse into a gaze. When people told John that Jesus's following was growing compared to his, John the Baptist replied, "The one who has the bride is the bridegroom. The friend of the bridegroom, who stands and hears him, rejoices greatly at the bridegroom's voice. Therefore this joy of mine is now complete. He must increase, but I must decrease" (John 3:29–30).

Jesus is the bridegroom. He's come to claim God's people for himself. This changes everything.

What's the Original?

In *Harry Potter and the Deathly Hallows,* Professor Dumbledore leaves Harry the sword of Gryffindor. But as the story progresses, we discover that a copy of the sword is being stored in the bank vault of the psychopathic witch Bellatrix LeStrange. The original sword has the magic properties needed to kill fragments of Lord Voldemort's soul. The copy does not.[2]

When we first stumble on the metaphor of marriage in the Bible, it's easy to assume that human marriage is the original and that it's just being used to illustrate God's faithful, passionate love for us. But if we read the Bible carefully, we'll find a counterintuitive truth. God's love for his people is the original. The greatest human romance is at best an imitation of that love. It can be beautiful, for sure. But like the copy of Gryffindor's sword, it doesn't have the vital, evil-killing power. So, if we treasure human marriage more than Jesus's love, we'll find it disappoints. But if we treasure Jesus's love above all else, we'll find it has the power to turn our weakness into death-defying strength. Toward the end of J. K. Rowling's book, the hapless Neville Longbottom stands up to Voldemort. He hasn't a hope of defeating this much greater wizard—until the sword of Gryffindor appears. This is the power of Jesus's love: a love that conquers evil and snatches us away from death. But if we grab onto this love, it also helps us live in love right now.

Like the deepest vaults in Gringotts's bank, the longing to be known and loved lies deep within us all. But Jesus is the only one who can fulfill that need. He knows every hair on our head, every fear in our heart, every word and every action: good and evil, cruel and kind. He knows the things we wish others would see and the things we're desperate to conceal. He knows it all, and despite it all, he loves you so much he came to die for you. Not just *people* in general, but *you*. I don't know your name. But Jesus does. I don't know your hopes, your fears, your hurts, your dreams. But Jesus

2 J. K. Rowling, *Harry Potter and the Deathly Hallows* (New York: Scolastic, 2009), 298.

does. Like a bridegroom awaiting his bride, he longs for you to be with him.

When we can see that Jesus's love for us is the original, it helps us understand both our deep craving for sexual and romantic love and our struggle to be satisfied with it. The craving can take different forms. For some, it's boundless sexual desire: the pull of Tinder, porn, one-night stands, affairs, or even serial relationships. For others, it's a longing for intense emotional connection—that person who gets us completely, who knows us from the inside out, who shares our every hope and dream. Modern, Western culture has lionized romantic love in novel ways. But its rip current has been felt by people in all cultures and across all recorded time.

"But soft, what light through yonder window breaks?" asks Shakespeare's Romeo. "It is the east and Juliet is the sun."[3] That feeling when the dawn breaks and everything around us changes, that feeling of intense burning, that desire to gaze at the sun when we know it will hurt our eyes and leave its impression even when they're shut, that's how young Romeo feels when he sees Juliet. But even as we see him kill himself to join his wife in death, we know this parched intensity won't last. What if the mail hadn't been too slow, and *Romeo and Juliet* had ended happily? If Shakespeare had written a sequel, we might have seen this couple grow in faithfulness, even as the thrill of "being in love" declined, or we might not. When Romeo first sees Juliet he asks,

> Did my heart love till now? Forswear it, sight!
> For I ne'er saw true beauty till this night.[4]

3 William Shakespeare, *Romeo and Juliet*, ed. G. Blakemore, Riverside Shaespeare (Boston, MA: Houghton Mifflin, 1974), 2.2.2–3.

4 Shakespeare, *Romeo and Juliet*, 1.5.52–53.

But hours before he was pining for another girl. His history suggests he might have found another woman beautiful as time went on. If truth be told, no single human love can hold us like the overwhelming power of the sun for long. It isn't meant to.

Don't get me wrong: God made romantic love to picture the intense, consuming, everlasting, sacrificial love that Jesus has for us. Good copies are still precious, even if they're not the masterpiece. And while Jesus's love holds the passion that usually wears off in human love, it also holds the depth we humans only surface over time.

Last week, as I was processing the 50-percent chance that I had cancer, I talked my husband through my fears about the ways that cancer treatment could devastate my body as much as the disease itself. I didn't ask, "Would you still love me if . . . ?" but he spoke to the fear he knew was lingering there and told me he'd still love me no matter what. I believed him. While how we look might trigger love at first, the best love burrows in until it works from the inside out. But Jesus sees us from the inside first. He sees us to the core and loves us still, however much we feel unlovable. It's not that he's blinded by love, as we can be. He sees our faults and lies and petty moral ugliness. But just as my husband's love could not be thwarted by my cancer, Jesus's love cannot be thwarted by our sin. Whether we are single or married, widowed or divorced, romantically fulfilled or disappointed, we'll all relate to human marriage best if we see it as a copy of the real thing—the love that truly burns for all eternity. And when we put this masterpiece in pride of place, we'll start to understand the Bible's boundaries around sex.

Why Is the Bible So Weird about Sex?

My favorite undergraduate professor was known for his provocative takes. He chain-smoked as he taught us and mocked me for my total lack of sexual experience. Gay himself and keen to expose us to all kinds of literature, he included comic ancient Roman gay short stories in our required reading. This was my first introduction into the colorful sex lives of wealthy men in ancient Rome. We saw in chapter 5 that Jesus taught hard things about sex. He condemned not just adultery but also all the other forms of sex outside male-female marriage. For Greeks and Romans, many forms of sex were A-OK: from things our culture condemns, like child abuse or sex with people you've enslaved, to things our culture affirms, like having a series of partners of either sex or committed gay relationships.

To be sure, this sexual freedom was reserved for wealthy men. Most women were expected to be chaste—unless they were enslaved or prostitutes. But wealthy men were free to sleep around. Gay relationships were sometimes frowned upon but were nonetheless expected. The Roman historian Suetonius commented that the emperor Claudius (who reigned in the decade after Jesus's death) was "immoderate in his passion for women, but wholly free from unnatural vice."[5] He meant that Claudius didn't sleep with men. But the fact that this was notable goes to show how normative gay relationships were. In fact, in Greco-Roman culture, the question wasn't whether your partner was female or male, but whether you were playing the active or the passive role. Sex asserted status, and being penetrated marked you as inferior. But Jesus took a very different view. Rather than sex asserting power *over* another person, Jesus said that sex creates oneness *with* another person.

One day, to try and catch him in his words, the Pharisees asked Jesus, "Is it lawful to divorce one's wife for any cause?" (Matt. 19:3). Some Jewish rabbis allowed divorce for any reason. Others only

5 Suetonius, *The Lives of the Caesars*, vol. 2, trans. J. C. Rolfe, Loeb Classical Library (Cambridge, MA: Harvard Univeristy Press, 1914), 65.

allowed it in cases of adultery. The casualties of the more permissive view were women, who could be abandoned freely. Jesus replied,

> Have you not read that he who created them from the beginning made them male and female, and said, "Therefore a man shall leave his father and his mother and hold fast to his wife, and the two shall become one flesh"? So they are no longer two but one flesh. What therefore God has joined together, let not man separate. (Matt. 19:4–6)

Jesus goes right back to the beginning of the Bible, when God creates us—"male and female"—in his image (Gen. 1:28). These are the first words the Bible says about humanity. They are also the first planks in the raft of human equality. We tend to see equality for men and women as a self-evident truth. But it's not. It started as a Judeo-Christian belief.

Jesus connects God's creation of male and female in Genesis 1 to a pivotal verse in Genesis 2. God makes man first, but then says, "It is not good that the man should be alone; I will make him a helper fit for him" (2:18). This role is not inferior. In the rest of the Old Testament, God himself is most often described as a helper. What's more, the creation of the woman is not an afterthought. In Genesis 1, humanity is told to "be fruitful and multiply and fill the earth and subdue it" (1:28). It's literally impossible for man to accomplish this mission without woman!

Right after God says he's going to make a helper, he brings the animals to the man and gives him the chance to name them. But no animal is a fit helper for the man (2:20). God does not discover this by trial and error. (Maybe an orangutan? Nope. How about a chimpanzee? Nope.) God had already made the animals before he said he'd make a helper for the man. Parading the animals before the man emphasizes that woman is different from them. Instead of being like an animal, she's like the man. To underscore this point, Genesis describes God putting the man to sleep, taking a part of his side—almost like taking a cutting from a plant—and making the woman. On seeing her, the man exclaims,

> This is at last bone of my bones
> and flesh of my flesh;
> she shall be called Woman,
> because she was taken out of man. (Gen. 2:23)

Just like in English, the Hebrew word for woman (*ishshah*) includes the word for man (*ish*). The first words God speaks about humans in the Bible were that he would make them—male and female—in his image. The first words a human speaks in the Bible celebrate the relationship between male and female. They're followed by the verse that Jesus quotes in his response to the Pharisees: "Therefore a man shall leave his father and his mother and hold fast to his wife, and they shall become one flesh" (Gen. 2:24).

Man and woman are cut from the same cloth. Marriage is in one sense a reunion, as man and woman become "one flesh." In case we missed the role of sex, the narrative concludes, "The man and his wife were both naked and were not ashamed" (2:25). This is the picture to which Jesus points when he's asked about divorce. If a husband and a wife are "no longer two but one flesh," if God himself has joined them together, then who are we to tear them apart? But we do.

Chimamanda Ngozi Adichie's powerful short story *Zikora* begins with a woman in labor. As the story and the labor progress, we see

Zikora texting the father of her baby. He was her long-term boyfriend who abandoned her when she declined his proposal—not of marriage, but of abortion. "I'll take care of everything," he'd said.[6] She'd told him she was stopping birth control and thought he was on board. But he had said they'd miscommunicated:

> "Kwame," I said finally, in a plea and a prayer, looking at him, loving him. Our conversation felt juvenile; an unreal air hung over us. I wanted to say, "I'm thirty-nine and you're thirty-seven, employed and stable, I have a key to your apartment, your clothes are in my closet, and I'm not sure what conversation we should be having but it shouldn't be this one."[7]

We find out later that Zikora had had an abortion at age nineteen. She was pregnant by a guy she'd met in college. "I don't do commitment," he had said, "but I didn't hear what he said," Zikora recalls, "I heard what I wanted to hear: he hadn't done commitment *yet*."[8] In the first century, poverty and fatherlessness often led to infants being left outside to die. Today, they are the biggest drivers of abortion—which is often less the flower of a woman's so-called right to choose and more a bitter fruit served up to women who feel like they don't have a choice.[9]

In some ways, the divorce of sex from marriage that we've witnessed in the twenty-first-century West is not unprecedented. Some form of commitment-free sex for men has been a feature of most societies throughout history, and women have borne the

6 Chimamanda Ngozi Adichie, *Zikora: A Short Story* (Seattle, WA: Amazon, 2020), Kindle.

7 Adichie, *Zikora*.

8 Adichie, *Zikora*.

9 For more on this, see Rebecca McLaughlin, *The Secular Creed: Engaging 5 Contemporary Claims* (Austin, TX: The Gospel Coalition, 2021), 75–80.

consequences: social, emotional, and physical. But Jesus locates sex in the one-flesh union of marriage between a man and a woman and gives it spiritual significance. This makes sense of his hard words about adultery and other forms of sexual immorality. Sex is not just a pleasurable act. It isn't even just a means for having kids. It's an expression of a one-flesh unity, made by God to picture Jesus's love for us.

The Pharisees ask Jesus, "Why then did Moses command one to give a certificate of divorce and to send her away?" (Matt. 19:7). Jesus replies, "Because of your hardness of heart Moses allowed you to divorce your wives, but from the beginning it was not so. And I say to you: whoever divorces his wife, except for sexual immorality, and marries another, commits adultery" (19:8–9). This teaching protected women and children from being abandoned. It presents marriage as a permanent commitment that can only be undone by adultery. As usual, Jesus takes what the Old Testament law said about sexual ethics and tightens it up. Even his own disciples are shocked (19:10). So why does Jesus—who never married—see marriage in these uncompromising terms? Because it is a picture of his own love for his church.

Whenever people ask me why Christians are so weird about sex, I first point out that we're weirder than they think. The fundamental reason why Christians believe that sex belongs only in the permanent bond of male-female marriage is because of the metaphor of Jesus's love for his church. It's a love in which two become one flesh. It is a love that connects across sameness and radical difference: the sameness of our shared humanity and the radical difference of Jesus from us. It's a love in which husbands are called not to exploit, abuse, or abandon their wives, but to love and sacrifice for them, as Jesus did for us. In Adichie's story, Zikora's college boyfriend often said, "'I don't do commitment' with a rhythm in his voice, as if miming a rap song."[10] With the same consistent rhythm in his teaching, life, and death, Jesus says to us, "I do."

But isn't it unjust and unfair for God to limit marriage to a man and a woman? Isn't same-sex love just as precious, deep, and lasting? Surprisingly, perhaps, the Bible answers "No" to the first question and "Yes" to the second.

No Greater Love

In *Harry Potter and the Deathly Hallows*, Harry is faced with a terrible choice. Voldemort has issued an ultimatum: unless Harry comes to the Forbidden Forest in one hour, he'll launch a full attack on Harry's friends. Harry could escape and leave his friends to face Lord Voldemort's assault. But he doesn't. Instead, he walks deliberately to death. But when Voldemort uses the killing curse against Harry, it only kills the part of Voldemort's own soul that lodged itself in Harry when he murdered Harry's mother. His mother's sacrifice of love has shielded Harry ever since. Now Harry's sacrifice can do the same. When he meets Voldemort again, they have this exchange:

> "You won't be able to kill any of them ever again. Don't you get it? I was ready to die to stop you from hurting these people—"
>
> "But you did not!"
>
> "—I meant to, and that's what did it. I've done what my mother did. They're protected from you."[11]

Harry lived because his mother died for him. Now Voldemort's attacks on Harry's friends are failing because Harry chose to die for them.

10 Adichie, *Zikora.*

11 Rowling, *Harry Potter and the Deathly Hallows*, 738.

Given how highly Jesus spoke of marriage, you'd think that he'd say it was the greatest human love. But on the night of his arrest, he said these stunning words to his disciples: "This is my commandment, that you love one another as I have loved you. Greater love has no one than this, that someone lay down his life for his friends" (John 15:12–13). For Jesus, friendship is no cheap knockoff of romantic love. No. The kind of sacrificial friendship-love that Harry showed is just as great as sexual and romantic love. And Jesus didn't only talk this way; he lived it.

The author of John's Gospel refers to himself as "the disciple whom Jesus loved" (John 21:20). This language has caused some to claim that Jesus was romantically connected with this man. But this hypothesis falls apart when we read John's Gospel as a whole. When two friends of Jesus—Mary and Martha—send him a message, "Lord, he whom you love is ill" (11:3), they're talking about their brother Lazarus. What's more, John goes on to emphasize Jesus's love for all these siblings: "Now Jesus loved Martha and her sister and Lazarus" (11:5). Jesus's love was not limited to his male disciples, but it included his female disciples as well. Later in John, when Jesus says, "Greater love has no one than this, that someone lay down his life for his friends," he continues, "You are my friends if you do what I command you" (15:13–14). This intense, self-sacrificing love, this love than which no other love is greater, is a love that Jesus has for *all* his followers and that he calls his followers to have for one another.

"A new commandment I give to you," Jesus said, "that you love one another: just as I have loved you, you also are to love one another. By this all people will know that you are my disciples, if you have love for one another" (13:34–35). Jesus's love spawns love in his disciples. Not a vague sentiment or fuzzy feeling—not erotic desire or intoxicating romance—but deep, life-giving, non-exclusive, sacrificial love. Like fireflies blinking in the dark, Jesus's disciples must be effervescent with his life-transforming love. For Christians, sexual love belongs in permanent, exclusive, male-female marriage. But this must not lead to an emaciated view of same-sex love. Rather, according to Jesus, friendship love can be as great a love as any.

This truth is deeply sweet to me. My teenage walls weren't plastered with pictures of boy bands. Instead, my heart was plastered with hopeless yearning for a series of girls. I thought I might grow out of it. I didn't. As every Christian (single or married) must, whatever their patterns of attraction, I've trusted Jesus with my sexuality. But while I'm married to a man I truly love, there will always be a piece of me that sometimes longs for something different, some elements of this desire that I must simply sacrifice. Romantic and erotic same-sex love is not what Jesus calls me to. But rather than depriving me of something that looks so good, he gives me something better: first, his own unstinting love that outruns any merely human romance and, second, the loving fellowship of other women.

I don't know how that strikes you. Perhaps you pity me. (If so, there is no need: I'm really very happy!) Maybe you think that my views are dangerous or that I'm just denying my true self. To some extent, I am. Jesus says we *must* deny ourselves or we can't follow him. But he also says whoever wants to save her life will lose it, but whoever loses her life for his sake will find it (see Matt. 16:24–25). And when I find true love in sisters in Christ, who know me and hold me and delight in me—despite my fear that once I'm known I won't be loved—it feels like finding life, like Jesus said. And even when it doesn't, in the moments when I feel the loss, the sense of grief at something I will never have, the yearning for exclusiveness that doesn't fit with friendship love, it makes me long for Jesus even more. You see, Christianity isn't designed for folks who are completely satisfied. It's not for people who have all they've ever wanted here and now. It's for the hungry and the sick, the longing and the lonely, the grieving and the failing—for the ones who know they're made for something more—because Jesus the bridegroom is still waiting for his bride.

Friend of Sinners

You'd think that given how highly Jesus thought of friendship, he'd be *really* careful in his choice of friends. You wouldn't want to die for just *anyone*. You'd want to know they were exceptionally good: that they were worth it. But Jesus took the opposite approach: he was "a friend of tax collectors and sinners" (Luke 7:34). Even his closest disciples were a bunch of moral failures. Right after Jesus gave them the commandment of love, Peter claimed that he would die for Jesus (John 13:34–37). But Jesus knew better: "Will you lay down your life for me?" he replied. "Truly, truly, I say to you, the rooster will not crow till you have denied me three times" (John 13:38). In Mark's account, based on Peter's own testimony, Peter claimed he'd stick with Jesus even if the others failed (Mark 14:29). But Jesus was right. That same night, Peter said three times he didn't even know Jesus

When they met after his resurrection, Jesus asked Peter, "Simon, son of John, do you love me more than these?" Peter replied, "Yes, Lord; you know that I love you." Jesus said to him, "Feed my lambs" (John 21:15). Then Jesus asked him again, "Simon, son of John, do you love me?" and Peter replied, "Yes, Lord; you know that I love you." Jesus answered, "Tend my sheep" (21:16). Then Jesus asked a third time, "Simon, son of John, do you love me?" Peter was grieved because Jesus has asked him three times. He answered,

"Lord, you know everything; you know that I love you" (21:17). Peter's three affirmations of his love for Jesus mirror the three times he denied he even knew Jesus. When the going got tough, Peter didn't lay down his life for Jesus. But Jesus laid down his life for Peter. And then—despite Peter's utter failure—Jesus made him a key leader in his church. Jesus is a friend of sinners through and through. His love for you and me will not give up.

So What?

In Yaa Gyasi's *Homegoing*, Ness is forced to watch her husband, Sam, be lynched. The horror of the scene speaks to the evil of her master and the system that enabled him to murder someone he'd enslaved. But it also speaks to Sam's unflinching love: for Ness, and for their son. To keep their baby safe, he dropped down from the tree where he was hiding and gave himself up to "the Devil." He knew he'd face a brutal death for trying to escape. But he was willing to endure that fate for love.

In Jesus we see a love so unrelenting that it drives him to the most excruciating death for us. We see a love that scoops up sinners of all kinds: tax collectors, prostitutes, so-called friends who let him down, disgraced women, religious zealots, and Roman soldiers. In Jesus, we see the bridegroom, who pledges eternal love and faithfulness to his people and proves it with his blood; and we see the friend, who calls us to love one another as he has loved us. In an Old Testament book called the Song of Songs (or the Song of Solomon), which celebrates romantic love, the woman at the center of the drama declares,

> love is strong as death,
>   jealousy is fierce as the grave.

Its flashes are flashes of fire,
the very flame of the LORD.
Many waters cannot quench love,
neither can floods drown it.
If a man offered for love
all the wealth of his house,
he would be utterly despised. (Song 8:6–7)

This is the kind of love that Jesus offers us. I want that love with all my heart. Do you?

7

Jesus the Servant

WHEN MAXIMUS first meets with Commodus in the arena, he kneels. It looks like an act of submission in the presence of the emperor. But then we see Maximus's hand in the dust quietly closing around a half-buried arrowhead. He's ready to kill the man who crucified his family—until Commodus's young nephew runs forward and stands in front of the emperor. Commodus praises Maximus and asks his name. "My name is Gladiator," Maximus replies and turns to walk away. "How dare you show your back to me, *slave*!" Commodus responds. "You will remove your helmet and tell me your name!"[1]

We've already seen how the Gospels present Jesus as the everlasting God and King. We've seen him as the mighty healer, life-transforming teacher, and unfathomable lover. But strangely, in the Gospels we can find another title for this inscrutable man, a role that seems at odds with all the other names he takes: Jesus the servant. Or even, in Commodus's terms, the slave. In this chapter, we'll

1 *Gladiator*, directed by Ridley Scott (Universal City: CA: DreamWorks Pictures, 2000).

explore this theme, and we'll see how Jesus's servanthood is part of how he conquers evil and flips the paradigms we thought we knew.

Behold, I Am the Lord's Servant

Early in the *Harry Potter* series, Harry finds a way to liberate the house elf Dobby. If house elves are presented with clothes by their masters, they're automatically freed. So Harry hides a sock in a book and gives the book to Dobby's cruel master, Lucius Malfoy. Malfoy passes it to Dobby. From this moment, Dobby is free.[2] But he's so intensely grateful that he's eager to serve Harry any way he can. Dobby's final act of service is to save Harry's life by rescuing Harry and his friends from Malfoy Manor. The evil Bellatrix Lestrange screams, "How dare you defy your masters?" But Dobby strikes back: "'Dobby has no master!' squealed the elf. 'Dobby is a free elf, and Dobby has come to save Harry Potter and his friends!'" He dies in the act. His last words as he gazes into Harry's eyes are, "Harry . . . Potter. . . ."[3]

For centuries before Jesus's birth, the Jews had looked back to the exodus as their great moment of release: "I AM WHO I AM" (Ex. 3:14) had set them free from slavery in Egypt. But they hadn't been released like helium balloons to float off aimlessly. They'd been set free to serve their Lord. The question for God's people was never whether they were servants, but whose servants they were. Would they live like Dobby, enslaved to people who oppressed and hated them? Or would they gladly serve the God who made and loved them?

By the time of Jesus's birth, the Israelites were living under foreign rule again. After many years of failing to serve God, they

2 J. K. Rowling, *Harry Potter and the Chamber of Secrets* (New York: Scolastic, 2016), 357.

3 J. K. Rowling, *Harry Potter and the Deathly Hallows* (New York: Scolastic, 2009), 474–76.

had faced his judgment and been exiled into Babylon. Thanks to another conquering emperor, they'd been allowed to return to their homeland. They'd even rebuilt the temple in Jerusalem. But they'd been through a succession of foreign overlords, and as the book of Nehemiah articulates, it felt like slavery: "Behold, we are slaves this day; in the land that you gave to our fathers to enjoy its fruit and its good gifts, behold, we are slaves" (Neh. 9:36). The Jews were in their land, but there was still a sense of homesickness. It was time for a new kind of exodus.

When an angel appeared to Mary, telling her she'd give birth to God's long-promised King, it was like the leaking of a secret intelligence file (Luke 1:26–33). "Operation Save God's People" had begun. The birth of the Christ was wonderfully good news of freedom for the Jews, who lived at that point under Roman rule. Yet, as with the first exodus, this message of release was not intended to let God's people revel in self-determination but once more to let them serve the Lord. Mary's last words to the angel express this perfectly: "Behold, I am the servant of the Lord; let it be to me according to your word" (1:38). The word she uses—*servant* (Greek, *doulē*)—could be translated "female slave."[4] She redeploys it in her famous poem of praise once she is pregnant: "My soul magnifies the Lord, and my spirit rejoices in God my Savior, for he has looked on the humble estate of his servant. For behold, from now on all generations will call me blessed" (1:46–48). For Dobby, serving Harry Potter is his greatest delight. For Mary, serving the Lord God her Savior is the ultimate blessing—even though it will

4 The old man who receives the infant Jesus in the temple uses the same word (the masculine form, *doulos*) for himself as he holds the baby in his arms: "Lord, now you are letting your servant depart in peace, according to your word; for my eyes have seen your salvation" (Luke 2:29–30).

mean immediate shame for her as the mother of a baby conceived outside of marriage.

With the infant Jesus in her womb, Mary rejoices in the utter reversal of servitude that God is setting in motion. In biblical prophecy, a past-tense verb can be used to speak of a future event to point to what God's certainly going to do[5]—like someone saying, "You're dead," to their antagonist before the fight. And so Mary declares,

> He has brought down the mighty from their thrones
> and exalted those of humble estate;
> he has filled the hungry with good things,
> and the rich he has sent away empty.
> He has helped his servant Israel,
> in remembrance of his mercy. (Luke 1:52–54)

In Mary's song of praise, we see two servants: Mary herself is God's *doulē*, and Israel is God's *pais*, which can mean "child" or "servant." In an act as radical as inverting Egypt's pyramids, God is instituting a new world order: kings will come crashing down from their thrones, and the lowly will rise up; the rich will go hungry, and the hungry will be filled; servants will be exalted, and masters will be humbled. The world will be turned upside down, and the master-slave division that cut right through the ancient world will be flipped.

When we think of slavery today, we likely think of the race-based chattel slavery that haunts American history and that was all too often enabled by church leaders. In the ancient world, slavery was pervasive. But it was generally not race based and often was not

5 Darrell L. Bock interprets the Greek verbs in Mary's song in this way in *Luke 1:1–9:50*, Baker Exegetical Commentary on the New Testament (Grand Rapids, MI: Baker Academic: 1994), 155.

permanent. People could sell themselves into slavery to escape destitution, and conversely people could sometimes buy themselves out of slavery. But slavery itself was seen as completely normal, and large numbers of people in the ancient world were enslaved. It was Christianity that challenged this way of thinking.

One of the first explicit arguments against slavery was made by the fourth-century church father Gregory of Nyssa, who argued from the Bible's claim that human beings are made in God's image that it was absurd to think they could be bought or sold: "How many obols for the image of God?" he asks sarcastically. "How many staters did you get for selling the God-formed man?"[6] This argument wasn't picked up by other Christian leaders right away. But by the seventh century, Christian abolitionism was taking hold, and over time the Christianization of Europe eliminated slavery in the West. This made the startup of the transatlantic slave trade all the more appalling. In addition to all the other ways in which the slave trade violated Christian ethics, it depended on manstealing—a practice specifically condemned both in the Old Testament and the New (Ex. 21:16; 1 Tim. 1:10). All the horrors of the ancient world were once again reborn under the auspices of supposedly Christian countries. But in the midst of the utterly unjust and anti-Christian system of abusive, race-based, chattel slavery, something quite extraordinary happened. Starting in the early eighteenth century, large numbers of enslaved Africans put their trust in Jesus.[7]

6 Gregory of Nyssa, *Homilies on Ecclesiastes* 4.1. Quoted by Kyle Harper, "Christianity and the Roots of Human Dignity in Late Antiquity," in *Christianity and Freedom*, vol. 1, *Historical Perspectives*, ed. Timothy Samuel Shah and Allen D. Hertzke, Cambridge Studies in Law and Christianity (Cambridge: Cambridge University Press, 2016), 133.

7 For more on the history of slavery and its relationship with Christianity, see "Doesn't the Bible Condone Slavery?" in Rebecca McLaughlin, *Confronting Christianity: 12 Hard Questions for the World's Largest Religion* (Wheaton, IL: Crossway, 2019), 175–92.

In its first centuries, Christianity had been so attractive to slaves that it was mocked by outsiders on this basis. A second-century Greek philosopher named Celsus quipped that Christians "want and are able to convince only the foolish, dishonorable and stupid, only slaves, women and little children."[8] So what was it that drew enslaved people to Christianity both in the second-century Roman Empire and in eighteenth-century America? Jesus. Despite the ways in which white slaveholders abused the Scriptures to try and justify their oppression, enslaved Africans in America came to realize that Jesus did not identify himself with the oppressors but with the oppressed, not with slaveholders but with slaves. Enslaved people were drawn to Jesus the servant, who throws down the powerful and lifts up the disempowered. As we read the Gospels, we find that Jesus is the driving force of a great revolution that had been brewing for hundreds of years, because he is both God's mighty King and his humble, suffering, sin-carrying servant.

Behold, My Servant

One of my favorite exhibits at the Boston Science Museum is a copy of the famous nineteenth-century optical illusion in which the same drawing can look like an ugly old woman or a beautiful young one. Sometimes I see one, sometimes the other, sometimes both—like a rotating mental door. If you read through the Old Testament book of Isaiah, you'll find you have a similar experience when it comes to God's servant. Isaiah points us to this enigmatic figure time and again. Sometimes it's sin-plagued Israel. Sometimes, it's a servant-hero taking Israel's sin upon himself. And as we read

8 See Michael J. Kruger, *Christianity at the Crossroads: How the Second Century Shaped the Future of the Church* (Downers Grove, IL: IVP Academic, 2018), 34–35 (quoting Origen, *Against Celsus* 3.44).

through the Gospels, we find they hum Isaiah's famous Servant Songs for us again and again.

John's Gospel quotes from one of the Servant Songs (Isa. 53:1–2) to explain why so many people didn't believe in Jesus:

> Though he had done so many signs before them, they still did not believe in him, so that the word spoken by the prophet Isaiah might be fulfilled:
>
> "Lord, who has believed what he heard from us,
> and to whom has the arm of the Lord been revealed?"
> (John 12:37–38)

Matthew quotes from later in this same Servant Song (Isa. 53:4) to interpret Jesus's healing work: "This was to fulfill what was spoken by the prophet Isaiah: 'He took our illnesses and bore our diseases'" (Matt. 8:17). Jesus the servant is identified with the rejected and the hurting.

In Luke, Jesus himself quotes from this Servant Song (Isa. 53:12) before his arrest: "For I tell you that this Scripture must be fulfilled in me: 'And he was numbered with the transgressors'" (Luke 22:37). These words in Isaiah are flanked by "he poured out his soul to death" and "yet he bore the sin of many, and makes intercession for the transgressors" (Isa. 53:12). Jesus is not a criminal, but he's treated like a criminal in his arrest. He asks the chief priests, who come for him with guards by night, "Have you come out as against a robber, with swords and clubs?" (Luke 22:52). Jesus is not a sinner, but he bears the sins of many and prays for sinners even as they are nailing him to the cross: "Father, forgive them, for they know not what they do" (Luke 23:34). If you're anything like me, you likely hate being falsely accused. Someone on Twitter this morning accused me of being disingenuous, and it rankled. I wanted to justify myself at once. Other people might be disingenuous, but not me! But Jesus takes the opposite approach, willingly wearing the sins of others like a shameful and humiliating cloak. Jesus is God's long-awaited servant, taking Israel's sin and suffering upon himself.

Matthew invokes another of Isaiah's Servant Songs to help us see who Jesus is. Keeping the Sabbath as a day of rest was clearly commanded in the Old Testament law, so the Pharisees try to trap Jesus with a question: "Is it lawful to heal on the Sabbath?" (Matt. 12:10). A man with a withered hand is standing in the synagogue. What will Jesus do? Heal the man and break the law, or leave the man and keep the Sabbath? Jesus responds by asking the Pharisees if they would rescue a sheep that had fallen into a pit on the Sabbath. He concludes, "Of how much more value is a man than sheep! So it is lawful to do good on the Sabbath" (12:12). Then he heals the man. But instead of rejoicing, the Pharisees are furious. They leave the synagogue and circle up to figure out how to get Jesus killed (12:14). Jesus knows what they are plotting, but he doesn't challenge them. Instead, he withdraws. But having seen his power, many follow him. Jesus heals them all and orders them "not to make him known" (12:15–16). Quoting from Isaiah 42:1–3, Matthew comments,

> This was to fulfill what was spoken by the prophet Isaiah:
>
> "Behold, my servant whom I have chosen,
> my beloved with whom my soul is well pleased.
> I will put my Spirit upon him,
> and he will proclaim justice to the Gentiles.

> He will not quarrel or cry aloud,
> nor will anyone hear his voice in the streets;
> a bruised reed he will not break,
> and a smoldering wick he will not quench,
> until he brings justice to victory;
> and in his name the Gentiles will hope."
> (Matt. 12:17–21)

Here we see a striking blend of gentleness and strength. God's servant will bring justice and hope—not just to the Jews but to the nations as well. He's not a typical conquering hero, careless of those he tramples on his way. Rather, he treats the hurt with tenderness. He won't let the bruised be broken or the sputtering get snuffed out. He doesn't raise a riot in the streets. Instead, he's filled with God's Spirit to bring justice for all. This is his victory. He is the Servant King, whose servanthood turns ugliness to beauty. And servanthood defines his kingdom. But even his closest disciples find this very hard to grasp.

Who Is the Greatest?

My family and I devoured the Tokyo Olympics. We got strangely into beach volleyball and synchronized diving. We cheered for Allyson Felix: five-time Olympian, most decorated American track and field athlete of all time, mother of a two-year-old, and open follower of Jesus. We delighted in Sydney McLaughlin: another Christian athlete whose name we're proud to share. But the biggest human-interest story was that of the outstanding US gymnast Simone Biles. Pre-Tokyo, she was already the greatest female gymnast of all time, and at the 2019 US Gymnastics Championships, she first sported a sparkly goat on the shoulder of her leotard. For Biles to claim she's the "Greatest of All Time" isn't arrogance. It's the truth. It remains true, despite the mental health experience that led her to pull out of most of her Tokyo events.

Unlike Biles or Felix or McLaughlin, we may not have the discipline or raw materials to be a world-class athlete. I certainly don't! But there is something deep within us all that craves the validation of success. Even in our smaller, social worlds, we like to be revered, to lift ourselves up and to push others down. A moment ago, after writing the sentence above, I clicked on the Twitter profile of a woman with whom I feel a mite competitive. She used to have many more followers than I had. Now, I have more than she does. I clicked on her profile specifically to check on this. I smiled in quiet triumph. It's pathetic, really. This woman is a Christian. Like Allyson Felix and Sydney McLaughlin, we're on the same team. I don't even see myself as generally competitive or caring about social media followings. My sinfulness is mostly weighted in other ways. And yet my ego was quite capable of crowing over her mere seconds after reading the teaching of Jesus we're about to explore. Perhaps you can identify. Give us even a little power, privilege, or prestige, and we're quick to lord it over others. Jesus's disciples were no exception.

Mark records an incident when Jesus had just warned his disciples—for the second time—of his impending death. The first time was after Peter had acknowledged Jesus as the Christ and then tried to persuade Jesus that he was *not* on track to death. Jesus had rebuked him fiercely: "Get behind me, Satan!" (Mark 8:33). Now, a second time, Jesus tells his disciples, "The Son of Man is going to be delivered into the hands of men, and they will kill him. And when he is killed, after three days he will rise." But his disciples "did not understand the saying, and were afraid to ask him" (Mark 9:31–32). Perhaps they remembered Jesus's reaction to Peter last time. But instead of discussing among themselves what Jesus might have meant, they spend their travel time debating quite another question.

When they get to Capernaum, Jesus asks them, "What were you discussing on the way?" (Mark 9:33). No one answered. "For on the way," Mark tells us, "they had argued with one another about who was the greatest" (9:34). That's right. Having just heard that Jesus was going to die, they spent their time, like kids on a playground, establishing a pecking order. Jesus reads his disciples like a disappointing book. He sits down and calls the twelve (his inner ring) to sit with him. Perhaps they wonder if he'll settle their debate. Maybe Peter is top dog, followed by James and John. But Jesus says the field's wide open. They're just competing in completely the wrong way. The contest isn't pole vaulting. It's diving. "If anyone would be first," Jesus says, "he must be last of all and servant of all" (9:35).

Did Jesus's message sink in? Not at all. The next time he predicts his death, he takes the twelve aside and warns them,

> See, we are going up to Jerusalem, and the Son of Man will be delivered over to the chief priests and the scribes, and they will condemn him to death and deliver him over to the Gentiles. And they will mock him and spit on him, and flog him and kill him. And after three days he will rise. (Mark 10:33–34)

The first time, it was Peter who said something stupid. This time, it's James and John. They come to Jesus privately and say, "Teacher, we want you to do for us whatever we ask of you" (10:35). Jesus replies, "What do you want me to do for you?" (10:36). They respond, "Grant us to sit, one at your right hand and one at your left, in your glory" (10:37). These brothers want the two top spots in Jesus's kingdom. But Jesus says they've no idea what they're requesting.

In language we'll explore in chapter 8, he says they're asking for excruciating suffering. The only way up in his kingdom is down.

When the other disciples hear what James and John have done, they're angry. How dare these brothers try to get ahead like that! But Jesus calls them all together once again to teach them the same lesson:

> You know that those who are considered rulers of the Gentiles lord it over them, and their great ones exercise authority over them. But it shall not be so among you. But whoever would be great among you must be your servant, and whoever would be first among you must be slave of all. For even the Son of Man came not to be served but to serve, and to give his life as a ransom for many. (Mark 10:42–45)

The Greek word translated "ransom" refers to the price paid to redeem a slave, a captive, or a firstborn (Lev. 25:51–52; Num. 18:15), or to make restitution for a crime or injury (Ex. 21:30; Num. 35:31–32). Traditionally, a king captured in battle might be ransomed by a great payment of money or an exchange of many less valuable prisoners. But here God's everlasting King announces the reverse exchange: he'll give his own life as a ransom for many.

I Volunteer as Tribute

In Suzanne Collins's dystopian series, *The Hunger Games*, a region in the Rocky Mountains has become the nation of Panem. The country's lavishly wealthy and high-tech Capitol is surrounded by twelve poor districts, which once upon a time rebelled against the Capitol. Each year, as a reminder of their subjugation, one twelve-to-eighteen-year-old boy and one girl from each district are chosen by lot to compete in the Hunger Games: a pseudo-gladiatorial contest that's televised for the entertainment of the Capitol residents. The contest is a battle to the death. When Katniss Everdeen's twelve-year-old sister Primrose is chosen as "tribute" from District 12, everyone knows what this means. She hasn't a hope against the likely older, better fed, more battle-ready teens from richer districts. But just as Primrose is about to be led off, Katniss shouts out, "I volunteer! I volunteer as tribute!"[9] In this desperate moment, she makes the choice to take her sister's place. When called on for applause, her fellow district members raise three fingers on one hand. Katniss (who narrates the book) explains, "It is an old and rarely used gesture of our district, occasionally seen at funerals. It means thanks, it means admiration, it means goodbye to someone you love."[10] Primrose would have no chance in the games. But Katniss doesn't have much more. The residents of District 12 all know she's going to her death.

Like Katniss, Jesus came from a subjugated group and offered himself to represent his people. Like Katniss, he's driven by love to volunteer his life in someone else's place. Like Katniss, Jesus ultimately wins and turns the power structure on its head. But unlike Katniss, Jesus always planned to die for us. And unlike Katniss, Jesus gives his life as a ransom for many (Mark 10:45). And unlike Primrose, we're not innocent. We're on our way to deaths we've earned. But Jesus volunteers to take our place. This is the key that opens up eternal life for us if we will only trust in him. But Jesus's stunning act of love is also an example: "whoever would be great among you," he says, "must be your servant, and whoever would be first among you must be slave of all" (Mark 10:43–44)

9 Suzanne Collins, *The Hunger Games* (New York: Scholastic, 2008), 22.

10 Collins, *Hunger Games*, 24.

The shock of Jesus's words here is lost on us because of how his teaching has shaped our thinking, whether we realize it or not. Like second-hand smokers, we've all inhaled enough of Christian ethics to think humility is virtuous. We relish tales of CEOs who spend time working on the shop floor or of film stars who make friends with extras. But Jesus's inverting of the power pyramid was truly radical.

Taking the Low Jobs

My husband and I are too cheap to buy an Apple TV+ subscription, so we binge-watched the first series of *Ted Lasso* with subscribing friends. The show follows an American football coach who is hired by a British football (aka soccer) team. The British soccer players are appalled and treat Ted Lasso with utmost contempt. But before he meets the team, Ted meets the kit man, Nathan. Ted asks his name. Nathan is stunned. No coach has ever asked his name before. As cleaner of the players' gear, he's insignificant. But Ted gives him the nickname "Nate the Great" and listens to his coaching takes.[11] In fact, Ted later promotes this kit man to assistant coach.

In Jesus's day, foot washing was a servant's job. It was a dirty business and required kneeling down. Both the act and the way it was done accorded with the status of a slave. When Jesus gets up halfway through dinner with his disciples on the night of his arrest, they might have thought he'd make a speech. Instead, he starts stripping down. He ties a towel around his waist—like any common servant would—pours water in a basin, and begins to wash their feet. When Jesus comes to Peter, Peter asks, "Lord, do you wash my feet?" and Jesus answers, "What I am doing you do

11 *Ted Lasso*, series 1, episode 1, "Pilot," written by Jason Sudeikis and Bill Lawrence, aired August 14, 2020, on Apple TV+.

not understand now, but afterward you will understand" (John 13:6–7). Peter pushes back: "You shall never wash my feet." He's horrified Jesus would serve him like this. But Jesus answers, "If I do not wash you, you have no share with me" (13:8). Peter, ever eager, flexes: "Lord, not my feet only but also my hands and my head!" (13:9). Jesus responds, "The one who has bathed does not need to wash, except for his feet, but is completely clean" (13:10).

When he finishes washing their feet, Jesus puts his clothes on again, returns to his place, and asks, "Do you understand what I have done to you?" (John 13:12). They don't. So he explains:

> You call me Teacher and Lord, and you are right, for so I am. If I then, your Lord and Teacher, have washed your feet, you also ought to wash one another's feet. For I have given you an example, that you also should do just as I have done to you. Truly, truly, I say to you, a servant is not greater than his master, nor is a messenger greater than the one who sent him. If you know these things, blessed are you if you do them. (13:13–17)

Thank God, we don't divide the world into masters and slaves anymore. On paper, we believe in equity. And yet we strive for status constantly, like players on a middling soccer team. Our pecking order currencies might vary tribe by tribe. A friend who lived in New York City before moving to Boston once told me that when you meet someone in Manhattan, you ask where they live, so you can determine how much they earn, while in Boston, you ask where they studied. One social group might value looks while another trades in athleticism. But put us humans in a room, and we'll soon sense our place and start to jostle. We might do this by sucking up or by kicking down. Two junior members of Ted Lasso's team were bullying Nate because they wanted to impress the star. But Jesus cuts through all of this. He takes the lowest place and serves. Whoever wants to follow him must turn his or her status instinct on its head and do the same, because he is the one who came not to be served, but to serve: both in his life and in his death.

A Slave's Death

In the preface of *Dominion: How the Christian Revolution Remade the World*, historian Tom Holland attempts to help us understand what crucifixion meant:

> Exposed to public view like slabs of meat hung from a market stall, troublesome slaves were nailed to crosses. . . . No death was more excruciating, more contemptible, than crucifixion. To be hung naked, "long in agony, swelling with ugly weals on shoulders and chest", helpless to beat away the clamorous birds: such a fate, Roman intellectuals agreed, was the worst imaginable.[12]

For Jesus's contemporaries, the cross carried the weight of the noose—only worse. "So foul was the carrion-reek of their disgrace," Holland explains, "that many felt tainted even by viewing a crucifixion." The noxious combination of agony and shame was what made crucifixion "so suitable a punishment for slaves."[13]

Other rebels could earn crucifixion too. As we saw in chapter 1, in 4 BC the Romans crucified about two thousand Jews who had rebelled against their rule near Jesus's hometown.[14] But just as the

12 Tom Holland, *Dominion: How the Christian Revolution Remade the World* (New York: Basic, 2019), 2 (quoted material is from the first-century Roman philosopher Seneca).

13 Holland, *Dominion*, 2.

14 The Jewish historian Josephus reports this in his *Jewish Antiquities* 17.10.

noose in America evokes the horrific history of lynching during slavery and segregation, so the cross evoked the death of the enslaved. For Jews awaiting God's Messiah, it was the last fate they would want for their leader. They longed for a victorious king, not a vanquished slave.

Meanwhile, for Greeks and Romans, Jesus's crucifixion would have proved beyond the smallest doubt that he was not divine. Successful emperors might have a shot at being recognized as gods. But as Holland explains, divinity "was for the very greatest of the great: for victors, and heroes, and kings." It was for conquerors with power to crucify, not crucified slaves. "That a man who had himself been crucified might be hailed as a god," Holland writes, "could not help but be seen by people everywhere across the Roman world as scandalous, obscene, grotesque."[15] But if you read the Gospels carefully, you'll find that death on a cross was not an aberration for the man who claimed he was the maker of the universe. It was the culmination of life in which he gladly played the part of the enslaved and willingly identified himself as Yahweh's servant.

So What?

If God himself has died for you, what more do you have to prove? If the creator of the universe loved you enough to give his life as ransom for yours, how precious does that make you? They say that something's only worth as much as someone is willing to pay for it. How much must Jesus value you and me to give his life up as our ransom? Jesus's sacrifice for us can breed humility if we will only let it. We won't need to be recognized by others if we know we are seen and known and deeply loved by the King of all the

15 Holland, *Dominion*, 6.

universe himself. We can unclench our grip on status if we know we're held in Jesus's hands. We can kneel down if we are sure that he will one day lift us up.

In the final movement of *Gladiator,* the Emperor Commodus decides to fight Maximus in the arena. He knows he couldn't beat him in an even contest, so he visits him in private first. Maximus is chained. Commodus taunts him: "The general who became a slave. The slave who became a gladiator. The gladiator who defied an emperor. Striking story! But now, the people want to know how the story ends. Only a famous death will do."[16] Commodus quietly slides a dagger into Maximus's back to weaken him before they fight. He wants the crowds who shouted, "Live! Live! Live! Live!" to see him kill their hero and prove his superiority. When Jesus kneels down like a slave and washes his disciples' feet, he's ready for the dagger in his back. He's ready for Judas's betrayal, Peter's denial, and the mocks and taunts of the religious leaders of his day. He's volunteered as tribute, and he's on his way to death. And only a slave's death will do.

16 *Gladiator*, directed by Ridley Scott.

8

Jesus the Sacrifice

CHARLES DICKENS'S *A Tale of Two Cities* weaves between London and Paris at the time of the French Revolution. The French regime before the revolution trampled on the poor in every sense. But the Reign of Terror that replaced it was no great salvation. Thousands of men, women, and children were hauled off to the guillotine without fair trial. In Dickens's novel, one of the unjustly condemned is a Frenchman: Charles Darnay. He's married to Lucie, whom the decadent London lawyer Sydney Carton also loves. So when Carton hears of Darnay's fate, he travels to Paris to take Darnay's place. The two men look alike, but on his way to the guillotine, Carton meets a poor, young seamstress who had met Darnay in prison and is now close enough to realize the exchange: "Are you dying for him?" she whispers. He replies, "And his wife and child. Hush! Yes."[1] Their whole conversation is so moving that I wept just now rereading it. Carton lived a selfish, drunken, disillusioned life. But now he dies a selfless death,

1 Charles Dickens, *A Tale of Two Cities* (New York: Signet, 2007), 365.

exchanging places with a man he hates, so the woman he loves can live in peace.

This chapter will focus on Jesus's sacrificial love: his willingness to die so we could live. The way that Carton's substitutionary sacrifice mimics Jesus's has often been observed. Like Jesus, Carton chose to die in someone else's place for love. But in this chapter, we'll also see how very different Jesus's sacrifice is.

Behold, the Lamb of God!

Carton first met Darnay when he represented him in a London court. Darnay stood accused of being a French spy, and Carton had got him off by pointing out how similar they looked. How could the witness know that it was Darnay he had seen and not Carton? Their likeness was how Carton saved Darnay twice: first in London, when he pointed out that he *could* be mistaken for Darnay, and then in Paris, when he *was*. Likewise, in the Bible, we see multiple moments in the Hebrew Scriptures that prefigure the exchange of Jesus's death.

In the first chapter of John's Gospel, John the Baptist sees his cousin Jesus and declares, "Behold, the Lamb of God, who takes away the sin of the world!" (John 1:29). To us, this claim makes little sense. We understand calling someone "the GOAT" but not "the Lamb"! But John's first Jewish hearers would have understood.

The first time God used a lamb to save his people was at the very start of their story. Abraham and Sarah were old and childless. But God promised to make Abraham into a great nation, and eventually Sarah gave birth to their son, Isaac. The name Isaac means "he laughs," so you'd think his birth would be the happy ending. But some years later, God speaks these devastating words to Abraham:

"Take your son, your only son Isaac, whom you love, and go to the land of Moriah, and offer him there as a burnt offering on one of the mountains of which I shall tell you" (Gen. 22:2).

Two months ago, I went to a lakeside beach with a friend. My nine- and eleven-year-olds can swim, but my two-year-old (Luke Isaac) can't. So I put his floaties on and let him run off with the girls. Before long, he got cold and came back to snuggle. I removed his floaties. Once Luke was warm and dry, he wanted to go back in. I thought I'd watch him, so I didn't put his floaties on. But soon I got absorbed in conversation with my friend. Suddenly, I realized I'd lost track of Luke. It was one of the first hot days of summer, and the beach was crowded with laughing, splashing kids. I could not see my son. I ran to the water and scanned it, panic mounting. I knew that even if I shouted for every person on that beach to look, they wouldn't hear. Then I saw a woman carrying a crying Luke. "He was going under," she said, reproachfully. I took him in my arms and held him tight. My heart was bursting with relief and crushed with horror. For days I could not shake the sense of guilt that I had risked his little life by my neglect. Yet here is Abraham, called by God to take his son, his only son Isaac, whom he loves, and kill him in cold blood. When I was in college, a friend of mine who was not a Christian started reading the Bible. He stopped at this point. He simply couldn't countenance a God who'd ask a man to kill his son.

As the story of the Bible unfolds, we find Yahweh *hates* child sacrifice, which was often demanded by other so-called gods. "You shall not worship the Lord your God in that way," Moses declares, "for every abominable thing that the Lord hates they have done for their gods, for they even burn their sons and their daughters in the fire to their gods" (Deut. 12:31).[2] But Abraham doesn't know this yet.

In Genesis 18, Abraham pleaded with God for mercy on the people of Sodom. But when God tells Abraham to sacrifice his son, he doesn't plead. He gets up early, saddles his donkey, and sets off. When they come to the mountain, Abraham has Isaac carry the wood for the sacrifice, while he brings the fire and the knife. Then they have this poignant exchange in Genesis 22:7–8:

> Isaac. My father!
> Abraham. Here I am, my son.
> Isaac. Behold, the fire and the wood, but where is the lamb for a burnt offering?
> Abraham. God will provide for himself the lamb for a burnt offering, my son.

We can only imagine what is going through Abraham's head. In Chimamanda Ngozi Adichie's short story *Zikora*, a mother gazes at her newborn son and thinks, "I would die for him. I thought this with a new wonder because I knew it to be true; something that had never been true in my life now suddenly was true. I would die for him."[3] No doubt, Abraham experienced the same true love for Isaac: his son, his only son, whom he loved. But he trusted that God would provide a lamb somehow.

When they get to the mountain, Abraham sets up the sacrifice. He binds his son and lays him on the wood. We don't know Isaac's age, but he's old enough to carry enough wood to burn his body up. Presumably, he could have fought his aged father if he chose.

2 See also Lev. 20:2–5; Ps. 106:37–38; Jer. 7:31; Ezek 16:20–21.

3 Chimamanda Ngozi Adichie, *Zikora: A Short Story* (Seattle, WA: Amazon, 2020), Kindle.

Abraham lays Isaac on the woodpile and lifts the knife. But suddenly, the angel of the Lord calls out: "Do not lay your hand on the boy or do anything to him, for now I know that you fear God, seeing you have not withheld your son, your only son, from me" (Gen. 22:12). When Abraham looked up, he saw a ram caught in a thicket by its horns. He took the ram and sacrificed it to God instead.

What was the point of all of this? Did God not know that Abraham trusted him? Was he engaging in some pointless, psychological torture of the man he'd sworn to bless? I don't think so. The God of the Bible can see people's thoughts. The point was not for *him* to learn, but for *us*. Like a preliminary sketch of a masterpiece, we see here the first outline of the Bible's central image. We see a father who intensely loves his son but who is willing to give him up. We see God providing a substitute, so that God's people, embodied in Isaac, could live. We see God sparing Abraham's son—his only son, whom he loved—while setting the stage for not sparing his own beloved Son. We see the Bible's first depiction of the Lamb of God, who takes away the sin of the world. But not the last.

The Passover Lamb

In *The Zookeeper's Wife*, while the Jewish ghetto burns, Jan and Antonina share a Passover meal with the Jews they're sheltering. The original Passover is described in Exodus. God tells Moses about the final plague. The Lord was going to pass through the land, and the firstborn in every Egyptian house would die. But the Israelites would be safe if each family killed a lamb (either a young sheep or a goat) and daubed its blood on the door of their house. Just as God provided a ram to be sacrificed in place of

Abraham's son, now thousands of lambs are sacrificed in the place of thousands of firstborns.

Again, we must ask, "Why?" Surely, God knew which homes housed Israelites without seeing blood on the doors! God's explanation gives a hint: "The blood shall be a sign for you, on the houses where you are," he says. "And when I see the blood, I will pass over you, and no plague will befall you to destroy you" (Ex. 12:13). The blood is a sign for the Israelites, not God. And yet when God sees it, he spares them.

My nine-year-old recently started a store in her bedroom. She's selling goods and services, but rather than asking for actual cash, she's issued us with pieces of paper, representing various dollar amounts. I buy real lattes with fake money! When God had the Israelites daub the blood of a lamb on their doors, he was rescuing them both from slavery in Egypt and from the judgment of death each one of them truly deserved for their sin. But the death of the lambs was no more the real payment than my daughter's fake cash. It was a pointer to the payment that would come when God would send his Son, his only Son, whom he unfathomably loves: "the Lamb of God, who takes away the sin of the world" (John 1:29).

We likely all believe there's sin in the world. We might not use that language. But we see the horror and the heartbreak, the cruelty, violence, exploitation, and abuse. We may be more or less optimistic about the possibility of forging a world that isn't riddled with these things, but right now it's clear that humans have a problem with sin. For some of us, the fact that we ourselves are sinners is yet more self-evident. We know our moral failure like the back of our hand. If there was a painting in our attic that recorded all our sins, we know how ugly it would look. For others, the idea that we ourselves are sinners feels like an antiquated glove that just won't fit. "I'm certainly not perfect," you might think, "but I'm fundamentally a good person." If that's how you feel, you'll have little use for Jesus. As we saw in chapter 4, he hasn't come for folks who think they're good. But if you're ever startled by your own reactions in a situation, or stuck in a pattern you can't seem to break, or thinking thoughts you're deeply glad that no one else can see, you might start wondering if you need Jesus after all: a sacrificial Lamb to take away *your* sin.

In a season of profound regret, a friend once told me that she wished there was a way she could have her guilt removed—"but not by someone dying on a cross," she added. Perhaps, like her, you see the need; you just don't like the method. Perhaps, like her, you want forgiveness, but not from God. It's understandable. For many of us, God seems so far removed from things that really matter in our lives. We know we've sinned against others, but what does God have to do with that? But if God made us and created us for fellowship with him, if he defined what good and evil are, if he made every other human being too, he's no more irrelevant to our sin than the mother of a murdered child is irrelevant to the murderer's sin. God is offended when we hurt each other and when we turn our backs on him, and he holds the key to the forgiveness and freedom for which we long. From the first, God has been calling for his people to come home. And from the first, the door through which God's people enter has been daubed with the blood of a Lamb.

The Sacrificial Lamb

After the exodus, God called Moses up a mountain to receive the law, including a detailed description of a special "tent of meeting" (also called the tabernacle) that his people were to build. It would be their meeting place with God. But even while Moses was receiving this law, the Israelites were worshiping a golden calf. Their sin formed such a barrier between them and God that the place where they would meet with God could not just be a gold-encrusted portal into heaven. It had to be a place where sin could be addressed. Like a water purification plant, God set up processes to separate his people from the sewage of their sin and to enable them to live purely before him. As part of this elaborate system, each morning and each evening, at the entrance to the tabernacle, God's people were to sacrifice a lamb (Ex. 29:38–43). These sacrifices marked the doorway to their meeting place with God.

When John the Baptist says, "Behold, the Lamb of God, who takes away the sin of the world" (John 1:29), the substitute for Isaac, and the Passover, and the sacrificial system would have sprung up in his Jewish hearers' minds. Jesus in the Gospels is the sacrificial Lamb.

But he's also the temple.

Destroy This Temple

When the Israelites finally settled in their land, their third king, Solomon, built a temple in Jerusalem to replace the tabernacle. Resplendent on the temple mount, replete with gold and precious stones, a place of teaching, prayer, and sacrifice—of blood and smoke and fire—the temple was their meeting place with God. By the time of Jesus's birth, this first temple had been destroyed. But after seventy years in Babylon, the Jews had been allowed to come back to their land and to rebuild it. In the only story we have from Jesus's childhood, the twelve-year-old Jesus stays behind in the temple when his family has headed home after celebrating the Passover. It takes Mary and Joseph a whole day to realize Jesus isn't with the group. Three days later they find him in the temple, talking with the teachers. Mary asks, "Son, why have you treated us so?" (Luke 2:48). Jesus replies, "Why were you looking for me? Did you not know that I must be in my Father's house?" (2:49). The temple is more truly Jesus's home than Mary and Joseph's place in Nazareth. But when he goes there as an adult, it's a very different scene.

In a rare account of Jesus being angry, we see him make a whip to drive the money changers out of the temple. He overturns their tables, crying, "Do not make my Father's house a house of trade" (John 2:16). His audience is shocked: "What sign do you show us for doing these things?" they ask (2:18). Jesus answers, "Destroy this temple, and in three days I will raise it up" (2:19). "It has taken forty-six years to build this temple," they reply, "and will you raise it up in three days?" (2:20). But John explains: "He was speaking about the temple of his body. When therefore he was raised from the dead, his disciples remembered that he had said this, and they believed the Scripture and the word that Jesus had spoken" (2:21–22). So was Jesus just forging a deliberately confusing metaphor? No.

Last month I took a dear friend out to dinner for her birthday. Karolyn is Chinese-American, and she was craving soup dumplings. Although I love most Chinese food, I wasn't jazzed. The thought of dumplings floating around in soup did not appeal. But when they arrived, they looked completely dry. I wondered if we'd float them into soup ourselves. Then Karolyn explained: the soup is actually *inside* the dumplings. You bite the top off and suck it out. Just as I had thought soup dumplings were in soup, Jesus's hearers thought his body was contained in the temple. But actually, the temple was contained in Jesus's body. Jesus is the place where God's glory dwells, the place where we can meet with God himself. He is the sacrifice, who gave his life so we could live. But he's also the temple, where the sacrifice is made. Like architectural drawings, the sacrificial lambs were only sketches of the sacrifice to come, and the temple was only a sketch of the one in whom the holy God most truly lives (John 1:14). But Jesus isn't just the Lamb and the temple. He's also the shepherd.

The Good Shepherd

In the opening scene of the 2016 film *Collateral Beauty*, advertising CEO Howard Inlet explains that his strategy is driven by three things: "At the end of the day, we long for love. We wish we had more time. And we fear death." These three things, Howard claims, drive every human act. But then we see him three years later. His six-year-old daughter has died of cancer. It's destroyed him. In his lament at life, Howard writes letters to Love and Time and Death. To Death, he writes, "You're just pathetic and powerless middle management. You don't even have the authority to make a simple trade." Later, he explains what he meant: "When we realized our daughter was dying, I prayed. Not to God or the universe. But to Death. Take me. Leave my daughter."[4] Like Howard, Jesus volunteered to make the trade. But unlike Death in Howard's mind, Jesus wasn't middle management. He was completely in control. "I am the good shepherd," Jesus declared. "The good shepherd lays down his life for the sheep" (John 10:11).

As usual, Jesus's words form the summit of a mountain of Old Testament allusions. Psalm 23 begins, "The Lord is my shepherd; I shall not want" (Ps. 23:1), and goes on to explore the shepherd / sheep relationship between God and his people. Isaiah mines the same metaphor, declaring of the Lord,

4 *Collateral Beauty*, directed by David Frankel (Burbank, CA: New Line Cinema, 2016).

> He will tend his flock like a shepherd;
> he will gather the lambs in his arms;
> he will carry them in his bosom,
> and gently lead those that are with young. (Isa. 40:11)

Likewise, Jeremiah proclaims,

> He who scattered Israel will gather him,
> and will keep him as a shepherd keeps his flock.
> (Jer. 31:10)

God himself was Israel's true shepherd. But the metaphor strikes another note in the Servant Song of Isaiah 53. Describing God's suffering servant, Isaiah explains,

> All we like sheep have gone astray;
> we have turned—every one—to his own way
> and the LORD has laid on him
> the iniquity of us all. (Isa. 53:6)

Quoting from Zechariah 13:7 on the night he was betrayed, Jesus warned his disciples, "You will all fall away because of me this night. For it is written, 'I will strike the shepherd, and the sheep of the flock will be scattered'" (Matt. 26:31). Jesus has stepped into God's role as the true shepherd of his people. But he's also stepped into his people's place to take their punishment. He's both the shepherd and the sacrificial lamb.

A good shepherd in Jesus's day was ready to risk his life when wild animals attacked his flock. But Jesus isn't just ready to die. Like Sydney Carton, he's actively planning it: "I am the good shepherd.

I know my own and my own know me, just as the Father knows me and I know the Father; and I lay down my life for the sheep" (John 10:14–15). But shockingly, rather than being attacked by wild animals, Jesus will be struck by God himself. This may seem at first like the greatest injustice: an innocent victim dying for other people's sin. But while Jesus in the Gospels *is* innocent, if we put our trust in him, we're not *other* people, we're *his* people. Jesus is not an innocent bystander hauled in to pay for our crimes against God. He is the person-temple in whom God and humans meet. He is the one true God made flesh, who alone has the right to judge and the right to forgive sins. He is the good shepherd, who lays down his life for his sheep, and if we put our trust in him, we are joined to him as closely as our bodies are joined to our heads. There's no way to tear us apart. And Jesus pictured this for us the night he was betrayed to death.

This Is My Body, This Is My Blood

In the opening scene of *A Tale of Two Cities*, a barrel of wine spilled out onto the street. The destitute lick at it hungrily. But one man "scrawled upon a wall with his finger dipped in muddy wine-lees—*blood*." Dickens adds, "The time was to come, when that wine too would be spilled on the street-stones, and when the stain of it would be red upon many there."[5] We use the expression *having blood on one's hands* as a metaphor for guilt. But on the night Jesus was arrested, he told his friends to drink his blood—not as a proof of their guilt but as a means of forgiveness.

First, Jesus took the communal bread in his hands, ripped it up, and said, "Take, eat; this is my body" (Matt. 26:26). You can

5 Dickens, *A Tale of Two Cities*, 33.

imagine how his disciples felt. Here was their teacher, tearing something up and saying, "This is my body"—like the villain in a film who holds up a doll to his victim saying, "This is you," before he tears it limb from limb. But somehow it was worse. Jesus doesn't only tear the bread. He also tells his followers to eat it. His body will be ripped up like meat for them. Then Jesus takes the cup of wine that would be shared as part of the Passover feast and says, "Drink of it, all of you, for this is my blood of the covenant, which is poured out for many for the forgiveness of sins" (26:27–28).

Old Testament covenants were sealed with animal blood. This new covenant between God and his people would be sealed with Jesus's blood. It seems so alien to us. Why would our sin require blood sacrifice? If there were really a spiritual price to be paid, shouldn't it *just* be a spiritual payment—a bitcoin equivalent to concrete cash? But in the biblical story, our souls and bodies go together, as human beings—flesh and blood—are called into relationship with God. The Bible doesn't promise us immortal souls that float off into disembodied bliss. It promises us resurrection bodies. Likewise, the sacrifice required for sin is not just made on some ethereal plane. It's made in flesh and blood. And yet it was a spiritual sacrifice. We see this in another cup that Jesus spoke of on that night.

Take This Cup

In *A Tale of Two Cities*, Sydney Carton goes calmly to his death. We might expect the same from Jesus, who predicted his execution from the first. But the Gospels tell a different tale. After dinner, after washing their feet, after tearing the bread and pouring the cup, Jesus took his disciples to a garden called Gethsemane. He told most of them to sit and pray, but summoned Peter, James, and John to come with him. Then, Matthew tells us, Jesus "began to be sorrowful and troubled" (Matt. 26:37). He said to them, "My soul is very sorrowful, even to death; remain here, and watch with me" (26:38). Going a little further on, Jesus fell on his face and prayed. Time and again, people fell down on their faces before Jesus, begging for help. But here we see Jesus with his face upon the ground, "My Father," he begged, "if it be possible, let this cup pass from me; nevertheless, not as I will, but as you will" (26:39). Luke adds that "being in agony, he prayed more earnestly; and his sweat became like great drops of blood falling down to the ground" (Luke 22:44). What was this cup that Jesus dreaded so? Was it the cruel death of crucifixion, designed to maximize the torture and humiliation of its victims? No.

The Old Testament prophets speak of a cup of wrath that God pours out in judgment on the nations for their sin. The Lord says to Jeremiah, "Take from my hand this cup of the wine of wrath, and make all the nations to whom I send you drink it. They shall drink and stagger and be crazed because of the sword that I am sending among them" (Jer. 25:15–16). Shockingly, the first recipient is not a foreign nation, but Jerusalem herself. We see the same metaphor in Isaiah, though the message is more hopeful:

> Wake yourself, wake yourself,
> stand up, O Jerusalem,
> you who have drunk from the hand of the Lord
> the cup of his wrath,
> who have drunk to the dregs
> the bowl, the cup of staggering.

. . . .

> Thus says your Lord, the LORD,
> your God who pleads the cause of his people:
> "Behold, I have taken from your hand the cup of staggering;
> the bowl of my wrath you shall drink no more."
> (Isa. 51:17, 22)

Habakkuk 2:16 and Ezekiel 23:31 use the same metaphor, and one of the psalms warns,

> For in the hand of the LORD there is a cup
> with foaming wine, well mixed,
> and he pours out from it,
> and all the wicked of the earth
> shall drain it down to the dregs. (Ps. 75:8)

The cup of the Lord is the cup of his anger against sin. This is the cup that Jesus dreads to drink.

That night, Jesus stopped his disciples from attempting to defend him from arrest. The next day, he stood before the Jewish and Roman authorities, and refused to defend himself. We see no hint of fear as Jesus interacts with those who plan to execute him. Jesus is not a victim. He's a volunteer. His dread was not of crucifixion in itself, but of God's wrath. The cup poured out against entire nations was coming to his single human hands so that he could take away the sin of the world.

Why Have You Forsaken Me?

Unlike the swiftness of the guillotine, crucifixion was a slow-burn death. Its victims hung for hours to be mocked by humans, pecked by birds, and gradually asphyxiated. Nails through wrists and ankles tore their flesh as they raised themselves up to gasp for breath. Speaking while being crucified was hard. But there was time. So much excruciating time. As we saw in chapter 3, Jesus made a stunning promise to a criminal crucified next to him: "Today you will be with me in paradise" (Luke 23:43). He also talked with his mother and with the author of John's Gospel (John 19:26). But the most moving conversation Jesus had while being crucified was with his Father. Luke tells us that even as the soldiers were nailing him to the cross, Jesus prayed, "Father, forgive them, for they know not what they do" (Luke 23:34). But Matthew records these more troubling words: "'Eli, Eli, lema sabachthani?' that is, 'My God, my God, why have you forsaken me?'" (Matt. 27:46).

Even the language of these words is poignant. The Gospels were written in Greek, the lingua franca of the empire. But occasionally, they keep the (transliterated) Aramaic words of Jesus's mother tongue. When Jesus healed the twelve-year-old girl, he said, "'Talitha cumi,' which means, 'Little girl, I say to you, arise'" (Mark 5:41). When he healed a deaf man, he looked up to heaven and said, "'Ephphatha,' that is, 'Be opened'" (Mark 7:34). When Mark records Jesus's pleading with his Father in Gethsemane, he includes the Aramaic word for dad: "Abba, Father, all things are possible for you. Remove this cup from me. Yet not what I will, but what you will" (Mark 14:36). But Jesus's cry to his Father on the cross is the longest portion of Aramaic in the Gospels: "My God, my God, why have you forsaken me?"

Each time I've given birth, I've opted for an epidural. Hours into labor, I'm ready for the pain to stop. But to get an epidural, you have to sit completely still. You feel contractions coursing through your body while the doctors stick their needles in your back, and you can't move. Each time I've done this, I've whispered to myself my favorite psalm: "O Lord, you have searched me and known me!" it begins. "You know when I sit down and when I rise up" (Ps. 139:1–2). It helps me trust the Lord and manage the pain.

When Jesus cried, "My God, my God, why have you forsaken me?" he was also quoting the beginning of a psalm. But he wasn't just reciting it for comfort. He was fulfilling it. "Why are you so far from saving me, from the words of my groaning?" the psalmist goes on (Ps. 22:1). Jesus in this moment is enduring in his humanness the great outpouring of God's wrath on sin. He's drinking the cup of the Lord to the dregs: in other words, he's going to hell. The physical pain of crucifixion expressed the spiritual anguish. Like the "cruciatus curse" in *Harry Potter*, the cross meant utter agony. Jesus as a man was soaking up the righteous wrath of God against a world of sin. But he's not confused as he cries out, "My God, my God, why have you forsaken me?" Even as he calls out in his anguish to his Father, he's showing that this had always been the plan.

Matthew records the passersby who mocked Jesus, "wagging their heads and saying, 'You who would destroy the temple and rebuild it in three days, save yourself! If you are the Son of God, come down from the cross'" (Matt. 27:39–40). Likewise, King David in Psalm 22 laments,

> All who see me mock me,
>   they make mouths at me, they wag their heads,
> "He trusts in the Lord; let him deliver him;
>   let him rescue him, for he delights in him!" (Ps. 22:7)

The chief priests and scribes and elders laughed at Jesus in words that echo these: "He saved others; he cannot save himself. He is the King of Israel; let him come down now from the cross, and we will believe in him. He trusts in God; let God deliver him now, if he desires him. For he said, 'I am the Son of God'" (Matt. 27:42–43).

The pain of this prophetic psalm, written by Israel's archetypal king, is mirrored in King Jesus's anguish (see Ps. 22:14–17). Just as King David wrote of enemies casting lots (the ancient equivalent of tossing a coin) for his garments (Ps. 22:18), so the Roman soldiers cast lots for Jesus's clothes (Matt. 27:35). But after all the pain and the lament, King David turns to praise. The psalm concludes,

> Posterity shall serve him;
> it shall be told of the Lord to the coming generation;
> they shall come and proclaim his righteousness to a people
> yet unborn,
> that he has done it. (Ps. 22:30–31)

Luke records these final, tender words of Jesus: "Father, into your hands I commit my spirit!" (Luke 23:46). John records him saying, "It is finished" (John 19:30). Matthew and Mark don't give us Jesus's final words. They only say that Jesus uttered a loud cry. But at that moment, Matthew and Mark tell us, the curtain in the temple—the curtain that walled off the place where God was most intensely seen to dwell—was ripped from top to bottom (Matt. 27:50–51; Mark 15:37–38). Jesus the sacrifice had made a way for sinful folk like us to live with God. He is the Lamb, the temple, and the sacrificing Shepherd-King, who drank the cup and paid the godforsaken price for us to live in paradise with him.

So What?

Talk of God's wrath and blood and sacrifice offends our modern ears. We like the idea of a God of love. But a God who grasps a cup of wrath and pours it out upon his Son feels like an ancient aberration. And yet we live in a world of unspeakable horrors—of war and rape and murder and abuse. If there is a God, we wonder, why hasn't he come down to judge and put the world to rights. The Gospels tell us that he has. He's come down in the person of his Son, who came to save the world by taking all the judgment we deserve upon himself, and to start a moral revolution that is bending us toward justice.

About to face the guillotine, Sydney Carton says, "It is a far, far better thing that I do, than I have ever done; it is a far, far better rest that I go to than I have ever known."[6] He'd lived a sinful, selfish life, and now he dies a love-soaked death. But where Carton was dying for a better man than he was, Jesus, in his utter innocence, faced crucifixion for you and me—and for the criminal on the next-door cross, who put his trust in Jesus with his final breath. Carton chose the guillotine so the woman he loved could live in happiness with someone else. Jesus chose the cross so that the curtain could be torn and we could live eternally with him. He is the Lamb of God, who takes away the sin of the world. And he'll take our sin too, if we will only put our trust in him.

6 Dickens, *A Tale of Two Cities*, 386.

9

Jesus the Lord

IN MATT HAIG'S bestselling book, *The Midnight Library*, a British woman, Nora Seed, decides to end her life. In different ways, she's lost her parents, her fiancé, her brother, her best friend, and (earlier that day) her cat. She's just been fired from her low-paid job in a boring English town. The elderly neighbor whose medicine she was picking up has found another helper. Her life feels pointless, so she opts to end it. Like a balloon let go before the knot was tied, Nora's life has fizzled out. As a kid, she was a champion swimmer, but she gave it up because she couldn't take the stress. She started a band with her brother, but she pulled out of their breakthrough record deal. She was going to marry a man she loved, but she called the wedding off. She was going to move to Australia with her best friend, but she got cold feet. She'd dreamed of being a glaciologist, but she'd never followed through.

When Nora takes the overdose, she finds herself in a gigantic library. Her school librarian, Mrs. Elm, is also there and she explains to Nora that—except for her bursting "Book of Regrets"—each volume in this library is a life she might have lived. Nora can try out different versions of her present, born from different choices in her past. She'll stay in each new life until she's disappointed. Then, she'll land back in the library. Her chances will finally run out when her body in her "root life" fully dies.[1]

I don't know how you felt as I described this book. Perhaps you feel, like Nora, that life has slipped through your fingers. Perhaps you had big dreams of love or fame or unbelievable success, but now you find your life's quite ordinary and your "Book of Regrets" is full. Perhaps you feel excited for the years to come. Or maybe you're just trying to get through. In this last chapter, we'll look at Jesus's claim that he is Lord: both over all the universe and over each of us. Our culture tells us maximizing freedom is the path to joy: if only we have enough choice, we'll find our bliss! But Jesus offers us a different way: not following our dreams, but trusting him. And if we do, he promises a thing more real and true and beautiful than anything our hearts could crave.

In Him Was Life

The first book of Dickens's *A Tale of Two Cities* is titled, "Recalled to Life." A French doctor, Alexandre Manette, has spent eighteen years unjustly jailed. His daughter, Lucie, has been told he's dead. He's mostly lost his mind. But finally, Dr. Manette is rescued. At first, he's so unused to freedom he can hardly bear it. The only name he knows now is his prison cell: One Hundred and Five, North Tower. He craves the shoemaking he learned in jail. He cannot stand the daylight. But gradually, his daughter's love revives him. It's not that he was literally dead in prison. His body functioned. But his mind and heart were broken. He needed to be recalled to life.[2]

1 Matt Haig, *The Midnight Library* (New York: Viking, 2020).

2 Charles Dickens, *A Tale of Two Cities* (New York: Signet, 2007).

John's Gospel says of Jesus, "In him was life, and the life was the light of men. The light shines in the darkness, and the darkness has not overcome it" (John 1:4–5). The claim's not just that Jesus was alive, like you and me, but that he is the origin and source of life. As an unborn baby's life depends on his or her mother, so our lives depend on Jesus. Conversely, the uncompromising label the Bible slaps on us if we're living without Jesus is *dead.* Like Dr. Manette in his captivity, our hearts may be beating, but we are spiritually deceased. Or maybe our lives just haven't begun.

One night, a Jewish leader, Nicodemus, came to question Jesus. Jesus told him that to see God's kingdom Nicodemus must be "born again" (John 3:3). "How can a man be born when he is old?" Nicodemus wonders. "Can he enter a second time into his mother's womb and be born?" (3:4). Nicodemus missed the metaphor. Jesus was telling this well-respected leader of the Pharisees that his life hadn't even begun. For it to truly start, he must be reborn. This conversation flows into the Bible's most remembered verse: "For God so loved the world, that he gave his only Son, that whoever believes in him should not perish but have eternal life" (3:16). Jesus isn't offering a better life for now: a Midnight Library where we can switch into a version of our life in which we've made better choices in the past. He's offering eternal, unrelenting life with him. But do we really want eternal life?

Life without End?

Our first thought when we hear "eternal life" is just a life stretched out indefinitely. In Greek mythology, the god Apollo offered the Cumaean Sibyl anything she wanted if only she would sleep with him. Scooping a handful of sand, the Sibyl asked to live one year for every grain she held. Apollo granted the Sibyl's wish. But when she still refused to sleep with him, he took revenge by giving her extreme long life, but not eternal youth. As the Sibyl grew older, she withered and shrank. Eventually, she was so small she lived in a bottle. When asked what she most wanted, she confessed she longed for death. Unending life would soon become a curse to us. But as Howard Inlet in *Collateral Beauty* observes, "At the end of the day, we long for love. We wish we had more time. And we fear death."[3]

You may be like Lin-Manuel Miranda's Hamilton, who imagined death so much it felt like a memory. Or like Howard Inlet, forced to confront death by sudden or long-drawn-out loss. But for most of us, the knowledge that we'll die is something that we carry like a donor card. We know it's there and what it means, but we live as if we will not die—at least in youth and middle age. A doctor friend of mine told me how many times she's sat with even older patients as they process for the first time that they'll die. But no matter how hard we try to keep it tucked away with our detritus and old library cards, we know that death is there, awaiting us.

In Genesis, God made the first man out of dust, and when he sinned, God warned him,

> You are dust,
> and to dust you shall return. (Gen. 3:19)

In his stunning poem "The Waste Land," T. S. Eliot draws on that picture and describes our fear of death like this:

> There is shadow under this red rock,
> (Come in under the shadow of this red rock),

3 *Collateral Beauty*, directed by David Frankel (Burbank, CA: New Line Cinema, 2016).

> And I will show you something different from either
> Your shadow at morning striding behind you
> Or your shadow at evening rising to meet you;
> I will show you fear in a handful of dust.[4]

But Eliot's poem is also suffused with classical mythology, and this handful of dust must also recall the Sibyl's fateful wish. We fear to die. But we also fear to live if living only means continuing: our shadow at morning striding behind us, our shadow at evening rising to meet us, our health failing, our body shrinking, our mind unraveling, our pleasures fading. Eternal life could be a terrifying thing.

What if we did better than the Sibyl? What if we got unending life *and* youth *and* all the things we want? The TV show *The Good Place* posed this question. In its final episodes, the central couple—Eleanor and Chidi—got to be together in their perfect home. They traveled the world and got to master any skill they chose. The answer to their every wish was yes! But ultimately, Chidi chose to end his perfect life. He needed not to be.[5]

Is this what Jesus offers us: an all-we-can-eat buffet of hopes and dreams? No. Jesus doesn't promise us a life of perfect self-determination. He promises to bind us to himself: the Lord, the source of boundless, joyous, everlasting life. Chidi worries he's not interesting enough to keep Eleanor happy for all eternity. He's right. But if Jesus is the source of life, the maker of the universe, the one through whom all things have come to be, he is the only person who can give us not just everlasting life, but life in all its fullness. And that's what he claimed he'd come to do. "The thief comes only

4 T. S. Eliot, "The Waste Land," *The Criterion* 1, no. 1 (October 1922): 50–64.

5 *The Good Place*, season 4, episodes 13–14, "Whenever You're Ready," written by Michael Schur, aired January 30, 2020, on NBC.

to steal and kill and destroy," Jesus said. "I came that they may have life and have it abundantly" (John 10:10). Thinking we can understand eternal life with Jesus from our current experience is like holding a glass of water and thinking that we understand the sea.

I Am the Resurrection and the Life

Jesus dramatizes his life-giving power in one of my favorite Gospel accounts. His dear friends Mary and Martha send for Jesus because their brother Lazarus is sick. Jesus loves these siblings (John 11:5). But he deliberately waits until Lazarus is dead. Then he goes. Martha meets him with these words: "Lord, if you had been here, my brother would not have died. But even now I know that whatever you ask from God, God will give you" (11:21–22). Martha believes in Jesus's power to heal her brother, even though he's dead. But rather than rushing to Lazarus's tomb, Jesus replies, "Your brother will rise again" (11:23). Many Jews of Jesus's day believed that there would one day be a resurrection of the righteous, so Martha responds, "I know that he will rise again in the resurrection on the last day" (11:24). But she's clearly been clinging to the hope that Jesus—the great healer—will bring her brother back to life right now. Jesus looks into her grief-struck eyes and says, "I am the resurrection and the life. Whoever believes in me, though he die, yet shall he live, and everyone who lives and believes in me shall never die. Do you believe this?" (11:25–26).

Almost all of Jesus's other "I am" statements are spoken to groups. This one is spoken to a single human being.[6] But even as Martha trusts him, Jesus shows her that she hasn't grasped who he is. It's not just that he raises the dead. He *is* the resurrection. It's not just

6 The other "I am" statement addressed to an individual is spoken to the Samaritan woman at the well (John 4:26).

that he offers life. He *is* the life. Martha starts to see it: "Yes, Lord," she replies. "I believe that you are the Christ, the Son of God, who is coming into the world" (11:27).

These death-defying words of Jesus haunt the final chapter of *A Tale of Two Cities*. Sydney Carton buys the drugs that will knock Charles Darnay out so he can take his place. Then he recalls his father's funeral:

> These solemn words, which had been read at his father's grave, arose in his mind as he went down the dark streets, among the heavy shadows, with the moon and the clouds sailing on high above him. "I am the resurrection and the life, saith the Lord: he that believeth in me, though he were dead, yet shall he live: and whosoever liveth and believeth in me, shall never die."[7]

Unlike Nora Seed, Sydney Carton is not dying because his life feels meaningless. He has "the settled manner of a tired man, who had wandered and struggled and got lost, but who at length struck into his road and saw its end."[8] Like Nora, he has lost his way. But unlike her, he's struck into his road and seen its end: an end not of missed chances, but of resurrection life.

As Carton walks through gruesome, bloody, revolutionary Paris, he helps a little girl across a dangerous street and ponders Jesus's words again, "I am the resurrection and the life, saith the Lord: he that believeth in me, though he were dead, yet shall he live: and whosoever liveth and believeth in me, shall never die." Next, Carton watches a trading-boat glide by. "As its silent track in the water disappeared, the prayer that had broken up out of his heart

7 Dickens, *A Tale of Two Cities*, 323.

8 Dickens, *A Tale of Two Cities*, 323.

for a merciful consideration of all his poor blindnesses and errors, ended in the words, 'I am the resurrection and the life.'"[9]

At last, Carton shares his final moments with the poor, young seamstress, who had also been sentenced to the guillotine. They kiss and bless each other. Then he lets go of her little hand as the bloodthirsty spectators get ready to number off another execution:

> The spare hand does not tremble as he releases it; nothing worse than a sweet, bright constancy is in the patient face. She goes next before him—is gone; the knitting-women count Twenty-Two.
>
> "I am the Resurrection and the Life, saith the Lord: he that believeth in me, though he were dead, yet shall he live: and whosoever liveth and believeth in me shall never die."
>
> The murmuring of many voices, the upturning of many faces, the pressing on of many footsteps in the outskirts of the crowd, so that it swells forward in a mass, like one great heave of water, all flashes away. Twenty-Three.[10]

On leaving prison, Dr. Manette had to learn to change his number—One Hundred and Five, North Tower—back to his name. Here, Carton dies as number Twenty-Three that day. But he believes he's entering a new life better than the first. Like Martha, he is placing all his trust in Jesus's claim.

In John's Gospel, Jesus talks with Mary next. She falls down weeping at his feet and echoes her sister's words: "Lord, if you had been here, my brother would not have died" (John 11:32). When Jesus sees her weeping, he is deeply moved. He goes to Lazarus's

9 Dickens, *A Tale of Two Cities*, 324.

10 Dickens, *A Tale of Two Cities*, 385.

tomb, where he weeps too (11:35). He weeps with these two sisters, whom he loves, because his love is always personal. It's not just for people in general. It's for Mary and Martha, for you and for me. But Jesus can do more than weep with us. He has the mourners roll the tombstone back, and calls, "Lazarus, come out." And the man who was dead walked out, his graveclothes still wrapped round his body (11:43–44).

Perhaps you're thinking, "That's a lovely story. But there's zero chance it's actually true." Maybe you've enjoyed some of the Gospel stories in this book, like you've enjoyed the glimpses of *A Tale of Two Cities* or *The Midnight Library*. But the line between fact and fiction is drawn clearly in your mind, and Lazarus being recalled to life falls firmly on the fiction side. If that's your sense, your incredulity will likely be yet higher when it comes to the claim that Jesus himself was raised from the dead—not for a time, like Lazarus, but for eternity—and that he will one day raise his followers to everlasting life as well. Perhaps, like the famous British astrophysicist Steven Hawking, you think the idea of life after death is "a fairy story for people afraid of the dark."[11] But unlike a fairy story, Christianity hangs its hat on a historical claim: the claim that Jesus himself came back from the dead. So is there is any reason to believe this actually happened?

Did Jesus Rise Again?

In his 2019 book, *Outgrowing God: A Beginner's Guide*, Richard Dawkins recounts an urban myth about life-sized helium dolls floating into the sky and convincing a woman that people were being taken up into heaven. Dawkins cites this as an example of

11 Lydia Warren, "Stephen Hawking: 'Heaven is a fairy story for people afraid of the dark,'" *Daily Mail*, May 17, 2011, https://www.dailymail.co.uk.

how "an untrue story spreads because it's entertaining and fits with people's expectations or prejudices."[12] He goes on:

> Can you see how the same might have been true of stories of Jesus's miracles or his resurrection? Early recruits to the young religion of Christianity might have been especially eager to pass on stories and rumors about Jesus, without checking them for truth.[13]

But there are multiple problems with Dawkins's claim. First, without the resurrection there would be no young religion to gain early recruits. Christianity without the resurrection makes about as much sense as the story of *Romeo and Juliet* without Juliet! Second, if people were making up outlandish stories, we'd expect the most outlandish claim—that Jesus himself had risen from the dead—to crop up in the later writings about Jesus. But the resurrection claim is central to the earliest Christian texts.[14] Third, the resurrection *didn't* fit with people's expectations. Even Jesus's own disciples weren't expecting it. In fact, the Gospel accounts are riddled with their disbelief. You'd think that if Jesus's followers were making up the resurrection, they could have painted themselves in a better light! But they don't.

What's more, all four Gospels present women as the first witnesses of Jesus's resurrection. If you were fabricating a story for

12 Richard Dawkins, *Outgrowing God: A Beginner's Guide* (New York: Random House, 2019), 23–24.

13 Dawkins, *Outgrowing God*, 25.

14 For example, in the very first chapter of 1 Thessalonians, thought to be his earliest letter, Paul describes how the Thessalonians "turned to God from idols to serve the living and true God, and to wait for his Son from heaven, whom he raised from the dead, Jesus who delivers us from the wrath to come" (1 Thess. 1:9–10).

first-century ears, giving women this pivotal role would be shooting yourself in the foot. Women were not seen as reliable witnesses. According to Luke, even Jesus's male disciples didn't believe them: "Now it was Mary Magdalene and Joanna and Mary the mother of James and the other women with them who told these things to the apostles, but these words seemed to them an idle tale, and they did not believe them" (Luke 24:10–11). Despite his multiple predictions that he'd die and rise again, none of Jesus's disciples—male or female—took him at his word. But when early on the third day, a group of his female followers, who had seen where Jesus had been buried, went to tend his body, they found an empty tomb.

As I said in the introduction, my hope when you have finished this book is that you'll read a Gospel for yourself. I'd love it if you read all four! But if you do, you'll notice differences between the resurrection accounts. All four agree that the women were the first to witness Jesus's empty tomb, that they met with angels, and that Mary Magdalene was in the group. But each Gospel tells a somewhat different tale.

First, there are differences in names. Matthew cites "Mary Magdalene and the other Mary" (Matt. 28:1). Mark names "Mary Magdalene, Mary the mother of James, and Salome" (Mark 16:1). Luke names "Mary Magdalene and Joanna and Mary the mother of James" but says that there were other women too (Luke 24:10). John names only Mary Magdalene (John 20:1), but when she reports the empty tomb to Peter she speaks for a group: "They have taken the Lord out of the tomb, and we do not know where they have laid him" (John 20:2). Do these differences discredit the accounts? No.

As we saw in chapter 1, names in the Gospels point readers to eyewitnesses. The different names the Gospel writers give don't point to their confusion but to the people they relied on for their stories—people their first readers might have known. Mary was the most common name for Jewish women of that time and place, so it's a mark of authenticity that the Gospels feature multiple Marys: both in general and in the resurrection accounts. Salome, whom Luke includes, had the second most common female name among first-century Palestinian Jews. Luke also mentions Joanna, whom he named earlier in his Gospel as being among the many women who traveled with Jesus and provided for his ministry (Luke 8:1–3). The different names in the resurrection accounts don't point to fabrication but to authenticity. But what about the angels?

Matthew tells us that "an angel of the Lord descended from heaven and came and rolled back the stone and sat on it" before the women arrived (Matt. 28:2). Mark's women saw "a young man sitting on the right side, dressed in a white robe, and they were alarmed" (Mark 16:5). Luke says that "two men stood by them in dazzling apparel" (Luke 24:4). John describes "two angels in white, sitting where the body of Jesus had lain, one at the head and one at the feet" (John 20:12). So were these angels, or were they men in white? And were there two or only one?

First, we know the Gospel authors are selective. One may only mention the angel who has the speaking role, while another mentions both—just as a friend might ask me, "Who is speaking at the conference you're going to," and I might answer with the name of the speaker I'm most excited to hear, while knowing there are other speakers too. And although you might think you could tell the difference between an angel and a man dressed in white, in John we see Mary Magdalene having a conversation with two angels without seeming to realize that they're not human. "Woman, why are you weeping?" they ask. She replies, "They have taken away my Lord, and I do not know where they have laid him" (John 20:13). Then

Mary turns and sees Jesus himself. But she does not recognize him either (20:14).

The scene between Mary Magdalene and Jesus is unique to John. Perhaps the desire to highlight it explains why John's Gospel focuses his whole story on her. Jesus says, "Woman, why are you weeping? Whom are you seeking?" John tells us, almost comically, that Mary thinks he's the gardener. "Sir, if you have carried him away, tell me where you have laid him," she says, "and I will take him away" (20:15). Jesus simply responds with one word: "Mary." His voice saying her name is enough. She turns to him and says, "Rabboni!" which in Aramaic means "Teacher" (20:16). Jesus immediately gives her a job: "Do not cling to me," he says, "for I have not yet ascended to the Father; but go to my brothers and say to them, 'I am ascending to my Father and your Father, to my God and your God'" (20:17).

In all four Gospels, the women are told to report the resurrection to the apostles. In Matthew, Luke, and John, we see them do their job. But in what may be the original ending of Mark, we hear that the women "went out and fled from the tomb, for trembling and astonishment had seized them, and they said nothing to anyone, for they were afraid" (Mark 16:8). This seems like a contradiction with the other Gospels. But Richard Bauckham argues it's not. He suggests that this description does not mean the women did not pass the message on to the apostles, but that they didn't tell anyone else. He also points out that fear is the appropriate response to what they'd seen and heard.[15] Like stumbling upon a spot that's just been struck by lightning, to be a witness of the resurrection is a terrifying thing.

15 See Richard Bauckham, *Gospel Women: Studies of the Named Women in the Gospels* (Grand Rapids, MI: Eerdmans, 2002), 289–90.

Later that day, Jesus joins two of his disciples as they walk to another town. At first, like Mary Magdalene, they don't recognize their Lord. Jesus asks what they are talking about, and they're surprised he hasn't heard about Jesus of Nazareth: "Are you the only visitor to Jerusalem who does not know the things that have happened there in these days?" (Luke 24:18). They tell him about Jesus being crucified and then report what the women had said: "Moreover, some women of our company amazed us. They were at the tomb early in the morning, and when they did not find his body, they came back saying that they had even seen a vision of angels, who said that he was alive" (Luke 24:22–23). Jesus responds, "O foolish ones, and slow of heart to believe all that the prophets have spoken!" (Luke 24:25). He goes on to explain to them how the Old Testament Scriptures point to him. But they're not the only ones who are slow on the uptake. As we saw in chapter 2, Thomas refused to believe the testimony of all the other disciples until he saw Jesus with his own eyes. Then he worshiped him: "My Lord and my God!" (John 20:28). "Have you believed because you have seen me?" Jesus replies. "Blessed are those who have not seen and yet have believed" (John 20:29).

I wish I could call up a group of living witnesses of Jesus's resurrection and have them tell you that it really happened. But the Gospels were written down before those witnesses died out precisely so that we could hear their testimony. And Thomas's story reminds us that even eyewitness accounts would not be enough for many of us to believe this extraordinary claim. We can't, however, dismiss the possibility of the resurrection out of hand. Just as with the virgin birth, if there is a God who made the universe, it's not at all illogical to believe he could raise Jesus from the dead. It would actually be quite illogical not to. And just as with the virgin birth, believing in the resurrection is not unscientific. Science observes the regular features of nature, and a miracle like the resurrection does not claim to be a regular event. Some of the world's top scientists believe in the resurrection.

Former National Institutes for Health Director, Francis Collins, became a Christian in his twenties. He'd been raised in a nonreligious home, and by the time he'd got to grad school at Yale, he identified as an atheist. But then he witnessed an older, female patient, who was suffering severe and untreatable pain, calling out to Jesus in her distress, and he became intrigued. Eventually, after considerable research, he became a Christian. When asked in a PBS interview, "What do you do about miracles or an event such as the resurrection?" Collins replied,

> I'm a scientist. When someone says that event was a miracle, it's natural for me to be skeptical, because until one has exhausted natural explanations, it's probably not a good idea to say that was a miraculous event. The blooming of a flower is, in my mind, not a miracle. It's something that we can understand on the basis of molecular biology these days. But I do accept that in special moments God, who is supernatural, chooses to invade the natural world, and to us that appears as a miraculous event, and that includes especially the most important miracle for my faith, which is the literal resurrection of Jesus Christ from the dead.[16]

Jesus's first followers did not have the modern scientific knowledge Collins has. But they knew enough biology to know that dead people normally stay dead. The death of their leader had devastated

16 Bob Abernathy, "Dr. Francis S. Collins Interview," PBS, July 21, 2006, https://www.pbs.org.

them. But when they at last believed that he had indeed come back from death, it turned them from a little group of scared and traumatized disciples into a preaching team that turned a tiny Jewish sect into the most widespread belief system in the world. Just as scientists see evidence for the Big Bang in background, leftover radiation, so the ripples of the resurrection are still being felt in the universe today. So what difference does it make if Jesus rose again?

Does It Matter?

Last month I was invited to a book group by a Christian friend. She'd had the other members read my first book, *Confronting Christianity*, and then brought me along to chat with them. One member asked me, "Does it really matter if the resurrection happened, so long as Jesus brings you comfort?" I said, "Yes. It makes the difference between life and death." You see, if Jesus was physically raised from the dead, it shows that he has power over death—not just to elongate our lives but to give us everlasting, resurrection life with him. It shows that everything that Jesus said about our catastrophic sin and God's impending judgment on our sin is true, and that everything that Jesus says about God's unrelenting love for us is true as well.

The resurrection slices through the claim that all the world's religions say essentially the same thing. Jews, Buddhists, Hindus, atheists, and agnostics believe that Jesus died and stayed dead. Muslims believe that Jesus didn't die, but only seemed to, and was taken into heaven. Christians believe that Jesus died and was raised. This is the engine driving Christianity. If Jesus didn't rise, the Christian plane falls from the sky. But if he did, it changes everything. It shows that death is not the end but the beginning. As Jesus said, "Whoever would save his life will lose it, but whoever loses his life for my sake will find it" (Matt. 16:25). If Jesus wasn't resurrected, he's an egotistical fraud. But if he was resurrected, he is the universal, everlasting, death-defeating, sin-forgiving Lord.

Jesus the Lord

In the last movement of *The Midnight Library*, Nora opens the book of a near perfect life. She's a Cambridge professor studying her favorite philosopher, married to her ideal man, mothering a lovely four-year-old, and playing with a dog named Plato. But much as she wants to stay in *this* life, she realizes it's not *her* life. She hasn't taken all the steps to make it hers. So, finally, she goes back to her "root life"—where she had tried to kill herself—and starts to build it back again. Her life was just the same but also different:

> It was different because she no longer felt she was there simply to serve the dreams of other people. She no longer felt like she had to find sole fulfillment as some imaginary perfect daughter or sister or partner or wife or mother or employee or anything other than a human being, orbiting her own purpose, and answerable to herself.[17]

This captures our most modern impulses. Don't tie yourself to others' hopes and dreams! Don't subjugate your will! Just make some meaning for yourself and orbit around that. But as I read these lines in Matt Haig's book, I noticed a discrepancy. What had made Nora happy in her ideal, Cambridge life was *not* her independence. It was love. She'd realized, "You could soak up whole thunderstorms of applause, you could travel to the ends of

17 Haig, *The Midnight Library*, 284.

the Earth, you could be followed by millions on the internet, you could win Olympic medals, but this was all meaningless without love."[18] And love demands that we trade our independence for commitment to our loved ones' good.

Jesus calls his followers to give up self-determination. He says they must deny themselves, take up their cross, and follow him. He promises that life is found in loving him, not in following our dreams. After his resurrection, Jesus called his disciples to a mountain and declared,

> All authority in heaven and on earth has been given to me. Go therefore and make disciples of all nations, baptizing them in the name of the Father and of the Son and of the Holy Spirit, teaching them to observe all that I have commanded you. And behold, I am with you always, to the end of the age. (Matt. 28:18–20)

Jesus claims to be Lord not just of the Jewish people, not just of his disciples, not just of one region or religion, one country or continent, one ethnic tribe or racial group, but Lord of all. The one who took a slave's role, who washed his disciples' feet, who was mocked and stripped and crucified, now claims he has the right to rule in heaven and on earth. There is no millimeter of the universe, no moment of time, no man and no woman that Jesus does not rightly rule. The only question is: will we submit to him?

As we saw in chapter 3, the word translated "gospel" meant a message sent by a victorious emperor to his conquered lands. When Jesus tells his disciples to go and make disciples of all nations, he is sending out this message. He's conquered even death, so he's

18 Haig, *The Midnight Library*, 248.

the rightful King of all who are alive. We have the opportunity today to welcome him, our Maker and our Servant-King, our Healer, Teacher, Lover, Sacrifice, and Lord. Or else we can reject his rule—for now at least. Like Nora in *The Midnight Library*, our time to choose is running out.

So What?

When the doctor called to tell me I was cancer-free, it was the news I'd longed to hear. But if my biopsies had come back cancerous, it would not have been loving of her to lie. I might not have found out the truth for months or even years. But in the end, I'd know I'd slowly walked into a death I didn't need to die, because she hadn't told me the hard truth I didn't want to hear. If Jesus is the resurrected Lord, we can't go on with life as usual. The truth will turn our lives completely upside down. If we reject him, we will enter into everlasting judgment. But if we welcome him, we'll walk through death to life with him forevermore.

When Nora Seed was sucked back to the library from her perfect life, a fire began. The building was imploding, and she had to hide under a desk. But Mrs. Elm encouraged her to run and find the only book that wasn't going up in flames: the book of her "base life." When Nora opened it, the book was blank. She scribbled, "*Nora decided to live.*" But nothing happened. She tried, "*Nora was ready to live.*" Nothing. Eventually she wrote, "*I am alive,*" and those three words recalled her back to life.[19] The early Christians had three words by which they lived as well: "Jesus is Lord." If you can only let those words sink in, you'll find your life. For whoever wants to save her life will lose it. But whoever loses her life for Jesus's sake will find it.

19 Haig, *The Midnight Library*, 270–71.

Acknowledgments

I WROTE THIS BOOK partly for my own sake. Despite having been a Christian for as long as I can remember and having spent three years in seminary, I feel like I'm only in the foothills when it comes to the Gospels. Writing this book was a delightful opportunity for me to be confronted by Jesus afresh. If it has helped you half as much as it helped me, I'm thankful!

I'm very grateful to the Christian and non-Christian friends who read versions of this manuscript and gave me feedback, including Christine Beale, Christine Caine, Julia Rosenbloom, Paige Brooks, Rachel Chaing, Ryan McElroy, Adriana Flores, Colleen Funk, Kristin Josti, and Deborah Choffi. I'm also thankful for my assistant, Joanna Beasley, who helped with the study guide that accompanies this book, and who continually saves me from my own disorganization.

Chris Cowan at Crossway was an excellent formal editor and helped me root out errors. Nathan Ridlehoover and Jonathan Pennington were kind enough to run their expert eyes over a draft of the manuscript and give me feedback. Any remaining errors are my own.

I'm thankful for Collin Hanson at the Gospel Coalition and Samuel James at Crossway for their continuing support of my work, and to Lauren Susanto and the Crossway marketing team for all their help in getting this book into your hands.

Rachel Gilson continues to be my first reader and greatest writing support. She also keeps me humble. Having a best friend who has been a Christian half as long as you have, but who knows the Bible twice as well, is a tremendous antidote to pride.

My husband Bryan and my children, Miranda, Eliza, and Luke, kept me grounded as I wrote and well supplied with both affection and distraction. I'm deeply thankful for their daily presence in my life. When I said I was thinking of going to seminary, my then pastor (whom I loved) asked me if I realized this would mean I wouldn't get married. "You're already very intimidating to Christian men," he told me. "This will only make it worse." I said, "That's OK with me. I just want to serve the Lord as best I can." Neither of us had accounted for Bryan.

General Index

Scripture Index

Also Available from Rebecca McLaughlin

"In this book, Rebecca McLaughlin takes seriously both the Bible and the questions of nonbelievers. If you're a non-Christian and have wondered why Christians think and do as they do, this book will be a good start to exploring those questions. If you're a believer, this book will not only equip you intellectually but also call you to compassion and empathy for your questioning, unbelieving neighbor, as well as prepare you to bear witness to the Light that has come into the world."

RUSSELL MOORE

Public Theologian, Christianity Today; Director,
Christianity Today's Public Theology Project

For more information, visit **crossway.org**.

More *Confronting Jesus* Resources

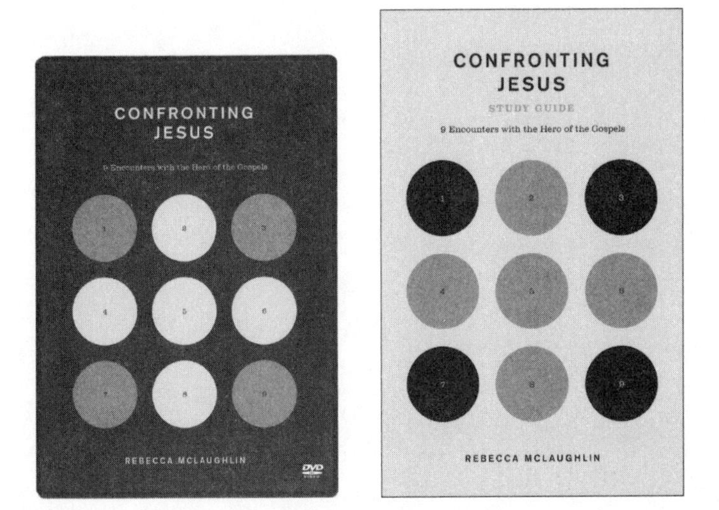

In the ***Confronting Jesus Video Study***, Rebecca McLaughlin hosts one brief segment for each of the book's 9 chapters, as well as an introduction and conclusion. These videos—ideal for individuals, small groups, and churches—are an engaging invitation to learn more about the person and work of Christ.

The ***Confronting Jesus Study Guide*** sparks further discussion about the historical and biblical facts in each chapter of *Confronting Jesus*, helping readers better understand the Gospels.

For more information, visit **crossway.org**.